CORPORATE HOSTAGES

ROADS TO CAPTIVITY, PATHS TO LIBERATION

N. Raj Mohan

RUPA

Published by
Rupa Publications India Pvt. Ltd 2025
161-B/4, Gulmohar House,
Yusuf Sarai Community Centre,
New Delhi 110049

Sales centres:
Bengaluru Chennai
Hyderabad Kolkata Mumbai

P-ISBN: 978-93-7003-525-6
E-ISBN: 978-93-7003-568-3

First impression 2025

10 9 8 7 6 5 4 3 2 1

Printed in India

CORPORATE HOSTAGES

Dr N. Raj Mohan is a seasoned coach with over 40 years of experience in Self and Organizational Development, working with Fortune 500 firms and leading corporates across India. His expertise spans leadership development, ethical HR, team building, and behavioural sciences, enriched by practices like transactional analysis, psychodrama, and Zen-inspired learning. He has designed leadership interventions, coached teams through transitions, and trained certified trainers across sectors. A passionate faculty and parental coach, he has conducted workshops globally and spoken at universities in Dallas and Lisbon. With over one lakh beneficiaries, he has also served on academic boards, authored four books and a novel, and appeared on television. He is the co-founder of BODHI, a firm focused on psychometric assessment, training, and career development.

For all those executives
who unfailingly remain humane themselves,
and towards others

Contents

Part IV
Liberation

Introduction

Mahabalipuram in Tamil Nadu, South India, has always held a special place in my heart. It was to a resort here that I would bring my wife and kids for almost weekly visits and watch my children frolic in the breezy ocean. The same town gave birth to the numerous thoughts I have had over the years. As my children grew up, the frequency of my visits here with my family reduced. But Mahabalipuram remained my reflective space, as I conducted several training sessions here for various companies. It was during one such OD (organizational development) interventional training session that I felt compelled to write a book about hostages within the corporate world.

During these training sessions I spent whatever free time I could find gazing at the ocean. The more I observed people on the beach, especially women, the more I started to see a pattern. Something about their joy seemed paradoxical to me. They wanted to be free, jump into the ocean, get wet, but their steps were always ambivalent, hesitant. I realized then that this was mostly due to the cultural standards many Indians are still bound by. Women can have fun, but they should be cautious. They can play on the beach, step into the water, but avoid exposing their legs. They can enjoy themselves but cannot allow their enjoyment to provoke the leering gazes of other men. They crib, but they also enjoy themselves—a dichotomy they have lived with for ages and many still do.

I started to draw parallels between how women on the beach in Mahabalipuram enjoyed themselves and how executives work in organizations. Granted, these scenarios couldn't be further apart, but the dichotomy these presented was evident. 'We want to, but we cannot,' has almost always been the 'reality' for several executives. While the sense of 'not able to do though I wanted to do' emerged strongly from various participants during my training programmes, they articulated their woes only when I reached out to them personally. Maybe the beach helped them get rid of their inhibitions and express themselves better, by discovering who they are, where they are and how they are!

I jotted down each of the recurring themes and patterns that I observed during the training sessions; all these added up to a long list of grievances. Listed below are the exact statements of several executives during my training programmes over the years:

> *'One has to compromise in order to climb the corporate ladder.'*
>
> *'I have to work in this company because I have already put in many years.'*
>
> *'I know I am missing my family but that is part of life.'*
>
> *'I am a workaholic, and there is nothing to do at home.'*
>
> *'I enjoy power and status here which other companies may not offer.'*

'I work here because this management will never sack us.'
'I do not like the company, but I am simply working here because of the salary I am offered.'

I realized these were not mere grievances, but echoes of their true feelings. The only metaphor I could assign to these troubled execs was that they were akin to birds aspiring to fly with clipped wings (who could never fly because their wings were clipped by the clouds).

The most important question I kept asking myself as a consultant was also the most obvious: Do hostage experiences exist across many companies? Do employers and employees hold the company to ransom as well?

I started connecting the dots. Also, around this time, the dreaded 'A' word—attrition—triggered a momentous discussion, formal and informal, on 'job visitors' among several executives. The attitude of these job visitors was comparable to that of honeybees—fly, land, collect nectar and leave—repeatedly disrupting the demand supply chain. (supply and demand of manpower). Moreover, it became increasingly evident that neither the potential employees nor the companies honoured the commitments they made to each other during job interviews.

The challenge of sustaining a competitive advantage in today's aggressive business environment preoccupies many business leaders. The bottom line is not 'revenue'; it is people and only people, as the wise leaders will attest. Retaining top talent was less of an issue in the past but the rapidly shifting grounds of the tacit employee-employer contract/understanding have given rise to new issues in the workplace. The old unspoken understanding commanded employees to:

- Work hard
- Be loyal
- Give all their time to the company
- Align with the owner or the top management's expectations

In return the employees would have:

- Accessibility to owner/top management
- A job for life
- A home away from home
- Tangible and intangible perks

The new tacit understanding is substantially redefined. Today's management is constantly fretting about employees staying on in the company, and is not sure how much they can share with them about the company's key financial and strategic decisions. A casual leave taken by an employee is viewed less as 'casual' and more as an excuse to appear for interviews at other companies, possibly with competitors.

Hence management follows a 'calculated' approach while dealing with employees, broadly bearing the following aspects in mind:

- *Treat any personal touch with employees as irrelevant.*
- *Do not invest in employees' training as there won't be any significant ROI.*
- *Squeeze the employees and get the best in the shortest possible time.*

- *Prevent employees leaving the organization from taking others with them.*
- *Ensure that the non-compete clause is fully honoured.*

Barring a few companies, the ongoing face-off between employers and employees is common and has lost its shock value. It has come to a point where both employees and employers have accepted these contextual developments as inevitable and have adjusted their strategies accordingly.

While there were many unspoken grievances on both sides, as I listened carefully, I heard a lot of concerns. Mostly these took on the form of helplessness, anger and desperation. Trust deficit between employees and employers has completely taken over the corporate milieu today and calls for immediate attention. Their collective voice resembles a blitzkrieg and the lament remains the same—I am being held captive and there are hardly any rescuers!

While this could be an alluring situation for some, there is a chunk of people who remain silent and wish they could free themselves from such 'hostage' situations. This book is for those who wish to be liberated.

▪

The manuscript for this book was finished before Covid-19 struck. Covid and the post-Covid era have redefined the meaning of life, more so within the employment landscape. These new experiences have taken the 'hostage' situation to a whole new level. Thus, it was important that I 'update' the book to reflect the changes ushered in by the pandemic.

As a response to Covid-19 in the organizational

context, the world witnessed the emergence and acceptance of 'Work from Home'(WFH). Various forums across the globe have debated the vicissitudes of Covid and its impact on the global economy, which is one of the reasons why I would like to restrict my observations to the relevant parts of this book.

The whole world has been deeply impacted, either directly or indirectly, by Covid. Survival of both employees and organizations today is a professional imperative, and it may not be out of place for me to say that one is being held hostage by the other. This effect, while visible across the corporate sector, has affected MSMEs (micro, small and medium enterprises) more deeply.

Against the backdrop of pre-and post-Covid-era experiences, at the very outset, I would like to indicate that I shall focus particularly on the following points:

1. Who are hostages, what are the different types of hostages, and what are their syndromes?
2. How are employees held hostage by their employers?
3. How has Covid added a different dimension to the hostage syndrome?
4. What are the strategies that can be adopted to liberate yourself from being/becoming a hostage?

While I explore the dynamics of being a hostage, the consequences and the liberating strategies, I must confess that a full understanding of the subject still remains elusive. This book is not the outcome of any research project; having worked with a myriad industries, people and levels, it is based more on the inferences that I have drawn from my experiences as a behavioural specialist and organizational development consultant.

The contents of this book are structured as a model inspired by the Buddha's Four Noble Truths and the Eightfold Path, believed to be delivered during his first sermon after his enlightenment. He declared that our life hinges on the following four foundations or truths:

1. The truth of suffering *(Dukkha)*
2. The truth of the cause of suffering *(Samudaya)*
3. The truth of the end of suffering *(Nirodha)*
4. The truth of the path that frees us from suffering *(Marga)*

He also said in the sermon that the Eightfold Path or the Middle Path that he had discovered, avoids extremes and can lead one to understanding, liberation and peace. It is the noble path of right understanding, right thought, right speech, right action, right livelihood, right effort, right mindfulness, and right concentration. I have followed this Noble Eightfold Path and have tried to realize understanding, liberation and peace.[1]

The word 'dukkha', suffering, often implies something negative, unfavourable—that life is full of suffering. Dukkha can have multiple meanings: incapable of being satisfied, incapable of bearing or withstanding anything, suffering, stressful. It can also refer to anything that is impermanent, temporary and conditional, or compounded of other things. It may equally imply something precious, experiential and enjoyable that will cease sooner or later.

---

[1]SN 12.65, 'Nagarsutta', Bhikkhu Sujato (trans.), *suttacentral.net*, https://tinyurl.com/4caza22k. Accessed on 6 May 2025.

The same essence or meanings can be attributed to the word 'hostage'. Feeling like a hostage is a part of our life and reality in that most of us define our work environment and career as stressful, unmotivating and uninspiring. This book discusses these four hostage situations in four parts:

1. How globalization and consumerism lay the foundation for hostage situations. (Chapters 1, 2)
2. Hostages: their definitions, types and syndromes (Chapters 3, 4)
3. Hostages' dilemmas, confusions and concerns (Chapter 5, 6, 7)
4. The Eightfold Path (strategies) to liberation from hostage situations (Chapters 8, 9)

This book does not aspire to or provide a path to enlightenment. It merely invites readers to reflect on its contents, and see whether following the eight paths discussed in it could liberate them from similar hostage situations. Those who have never been in such situations may also find this book useful.

Aristotle is believed to have said, 'Knowing yourself is the beginning of all wisdom.' Knowing yourself is truly the first step forward; thereafter, the long road to liberation doesn't matter.

Part I

Consumerism

The folly of endless consumerism sends us on a wild goose-chase for happiness through materialism.

—BRYANT H. MCGILL

1

Blaming it on the Globe

Accidents take place due to one of two reasons: an unsafe act or an unsafe condition. Oddly, accidents and hostage situations share a similarity. Even though a hostage situation is often premeditated or preplanned to an extent by the perpetrators, hostages, much like accident victims, are often unaware that they are going to be taken hostage.

Conversely, corporate hostages often invite themselves consciously and willingly into such situations. It is a deliberate attempt on their part to further their interests, guided by the principle 'no pain no gain.' It is also deemed as a 'quid pro quo.' Often the *quid* and *quo* are asymmetrical and imbalanced. Many a time, what one gains in lieu of the pain is irrational, irreversible, and mainly materialistic. As considerations of monetary and other gains draw several people into this captivity—and many remain trapped in this vicious cycle—a courageous few prefer to prioritize their well-being—mental and physical. Ironically, despite the disruption Covid-19 created and the wisdom it imparted, intense globalization and consumerism pre- and post-Covid have given rise to fierce competition among industries for their rightful share. Unfortunately, there has been a spike in competition for their rightful share among individuals too.

Dr Abbas Bakhtiar, an industry expert and author, observes: 'It is said that today is pregnant with tomorrow. What and how we have done things in the past have shaped our today, and what and how we do things today determine the shape of our future. To see into the future of our economies, with some small degree of certainty, we have to pay attention to what is happening around us and what we do.'[1]

Unfortunately, the term 'economy' often invites macro responses—rather than micro responses—from the common people. Our understanding of the world economy and its effects is rather dim compared to the importance we give to money. We feel 'handling' economics is the job of the government or banks, or business analysts, and we conveniently ignore its workings as if it were extraneous to us. The only time we ever relate to it is when we are faced with lay-offs, job cuts and pay cuts. The fact is, we refuse to take individual responsibility for creating a distressful economic situation.

Business is as interconnected as people and their objectives. In early 2009, the then International Monetary Fund's (IMF) chief Dominique Strauss Khanhad said, 'The world's advanced economic countries, i.e. the US, Europe, Japan and the Middle East, are already in depression.'[2]

---

[1]Bakhtiar, Dr Abbas, 'Global Economic Outlook: 2012 and Beyond', *The Market Oracle*, 23 February 2009, https://tinyurl.com/yyx86nps. Accessed on 6 May 2025.

[2]Davis, Bob, and Elffie Chew, 'IMF Chief Says Nations in "Depression"',

We have heard stories about expatriates relocating to their countries of origin, abandoning their automobiles at airports or public parking spaces. What's worse is that this situation persists in many countries even now, and they are yet to come to terms with it. The GDP of several countries is on a downward trend and shows little sign of recovery. When former US President Barack Obama struggled to address the economic distress plaguing the US, there was widespread panic in countries like India and China. The period under President Joe Biden was no different as the number of people who lost their jobs was high, and persons who completed temporary jobs increased by 3 million in May 2025.[3] The US's announcement on visa restrictions and tax relief to local companies gave a jolt to companies elsewhere. The situation has not eased up since President Trump has taken over, especially due to his latest trade policies.

After being re-elected President of the United States, 'Trump has led with cruelty and chaos creating human rights emergencies that have affected millions of people,'[4] said Paul O' Brien, Executive Director of Amnesty International, USA. Trump's executive orders on bilateral trade relationships with other countries, his disparate trade

---

The Wall Street Journal, 9 February 2009, https://tinyurl.com/46t2wrxz. Accessed on 6 May 2025

[3]*U.S. Bureau of Labor Statistics,* 'Employment Situation Summary of August 2025—,' *bls.gov,* 2 May 2025, https://tinyurl.com/4k7kczsc. Accessed on 6 May 2025

[4]*Amnesty International,* 'President Trump's First 100 Days: Attacks on Human Rights, Cruelty and Chaos,' *amnesty.org,* 30 April 2025, https://tinyurl.com/2judfy8v. Accessed on 30 May 2025.

tariffs, his restrictions on US H-1B visas and his decision to suspend students visas and deport illegal immigrants have sent shock waves around the world. The impact of an arbitrary decision of one country impacts the future of many others. A federal court has blocked President Trump from imposing sweeping tariffs on imports which have rocked global financial markets, resulting in unemployment and disruption in the world economy.[5] Many countries are yet to come to terms with the adverse conditions arising from such policies, with little idea of how long the resultant economic uncertainty may last, or how long the legal twists and entanglements may take to be resolved.

The expansionist policies of some countries and/or their desire to establish their business hegemony in the global economic order will always have a reaction. Such countries often face the destructive consequences of their own deeds, arrogance and political ambitions. Being caught in a double bind, this is akin to holding on to a tiger's tail—you can neither hold on for long nor can you let go. The same analogy is applicable to every entity, including a business, and at a microscopic level, even to an individual.

Long ago, I had the experience of meeting a raja. Although he is without a kingdom now, he is still revered as a raja by the people of a small community in South India. My entire idea of a raja was shattered when I met him—a well-educated man in his partially dilapidated palace.

---

[5]Cole, Devan, Katelyn Polantz, Ramishah Maruf, and Elisabeth Buchwald, 'Appeals court strikes down many Trump tariffs, but delays enforcement until October', *edition.cnn.com*, 29 August 2025. https://tinyurl.com/ar5mm54b. Accessed on 30 August 2025.

Perhaps with the better clothes on, I was embarrassed to sit in front of him. During our conversation, his eyes often became moist when he recounted his past—his horse-drawn chariots, his education abroad, how his father killed an arrogant British teacher with his rifle for his disparaging comments about Indians, and his once-extravagant lifestyle as a prince and a raja.

Finding me empathetic, he had no qualms about sharing how he was unable to make both ends meet. He also averred sadly but genuinely how he was living in the reflected glory of his past rather than in the present. The profligacy he indulged in as a chieftain, including during his daughter's marriage, trying to fulfil the needs of the subjects in his 'kingdom', heading all social functions, and trying to sustain an unrealistic lifestyle for his children, made him more a leader in exile from his own reality. His daily struggle between 'being' a raja and the reality of his present status repeatedly drove home the utter futility of pretension. In his own words, he was exasperated, saying he was a captive in his *own* prison.

Countries are no different than the raja I have mentioned. The overwhelming need to flaunt their supremacy and to try to sustain that impression, lest they be upstaged by others, makes them lose sight of the security, well-being, faith and trust of their own people.

Any reader of Alvin Toffler's *The Third Wave* (1980) will concur with me that most of the topics and themes discussed by him are relevant today. These 'waves' are described by Toffler as Agricultural, Industrial and Knowledge or Information. Although *The Third Wave* was written predominantly keeping America in mind, its relevance today—not just in developed but also in developing countries—is significant. The migration of labour, stringent immigration laws, racial animosity due to real and perceived prospect of job snatching, the impact of Covid, the advent of AI, and ChatGPT—all bear out Toffler's predictions.

Toffler writes, 'Whenever a single wave of change predominates in any given society, the pattern of future development is relatively easy to discern.'[6] In contrast, when a society is struck by two or more giant waves of change, and none is yet clearly dominant, the image of the future is fractured. It becomes extremely difficult to understand the meaning of the changes and conflicts that arise thereof. The collision of wave fronts creates a raging ocean, full of clashing currents, eddies, and maelstroms which conceal the deeper, more important historic tides. The collision of these waves creates social tensions, dangerous conflicts, and strange new political wave fronts that cut across the usual divides of class, race, sex or party. This collision reduces to shambles the traditional political vocabulary and makes it difficult to separate the progressives from the reactionaries, friends from enemies.

---

[6]Toffler, Alvin, 'Chapter 1: Super Struggle', *The Third Wave*, William Morrow and Company, Inc., New York, 1980, p. 31.

2

Complexities/Dynamics of Globalization in Indian Context

A scrutiny of today's commercial advertisements provides an interesting insight into consumerism. The stress is no longer on creating products for people; it is on creating people for products. This is essentially the defining feature of culture under globalization. Humans are systematically reduced to the status of products who will consume what is produced. This consumerism (de)generates its own atmosphere, which affects every aspect of our life and society. What better example than social media networking sites that literally sell our profiles, making us the product instead. It's no secret or coincidence that your interests are aligned with the advertisements you see on the websites you browse. Your habits, likes, dislikes, what you need or what you are shopping around for are all captured and passed on to social networking giants. A person's social media behaviour is closely watched and observed well enough to create algorithms and patterns to suit the individual. In absolute certain terms, our privacy has certainly been compromised allowing for full-fledged social tracking, in part due to unregulated online media governance. The downside of all this not just pertains to one's privacy but also makes us hostages who, unfortunately, are under threat all the time.

In the era of globalization, consumerism emerges as a connected output. Also, it won't be far-fetched to think that fierce competition and people's increasingly self-gratifying consumerism will wipe out certain basic foundations of their well-being. A detailed discussion on the 'good and bad' of globalization or consumerism is beyond the scope of this book. I am merely trying to draw the readers' attention to both perspectives, and how they affect our growth and well-being. I implore people to define 'growth' without being 'held captive' in the name of 'growth'.

That said, I must acknowledge that globalization has increasingly integrated people across the world by means of technology and trade and is a massive boon to humanity, permeating even our everyday conversation.

The internet knows no bounds. Today, it is convenient for anyone to communicate at will regularly with kith and kin across the globe, to overcome cultural barriers and forge friendships, and conduct businesses across borders, thereby allowing the world to become a more intimate, interesting *and* intimidating place to live in. The positives of globalization have been an integral part of India's recent economic progress, and played a major role in its export-led growth, leading to an expanding job market in the country.

One of the major benefits of globalization in India has been the growth in IT and business process outsourcing (BPO) services. Over the last few years, India has seen an increase in the number of skilled professionals in both sectors to service customers in the US and Europe. Taking advantage of the developing countries' low-cost but educated, English-speaking workforce, and utilizing global communications technologies such as email and the internet, international companies have been able to keep their cost base at a minimum by establishing outsourced knowledge-worker operations.

As a new Indian middle class develops its wealth from and around IT-related industries, a new consumer base has simultaneously been established. International companies have been expanding their operations as well to service this massive growth opportunity. Multinational bigwigs like McDonald's, KFC, Coca-Cola and Pepsi have set up shop and cater to the growing needs of an increasingly urban population. Auto giants like Hyundai, Toyota, KIA and BMW have been well accepted by Indians. This has been extremely advantageous to the multinationals. By simply increasing their base of operation, expanding their workforce with minimal investments, and providing services to a broad range of consumers, these multinationals have opened up many profitable opportunities within the Indian market.

In return for the many benefits that globalization has given India, companies owned/managed by Indians have rapidly gained confidence and are morphing into major players on the international scene. From telecom to films, from automobiles to IT, Indian companies are setting themselves up as powerhouses of tomorrow's global economy. This has considerably raised the bar of per capita income for Indians in urban areas.

This evolving economic reality raises some significant questions:

- Does this come at a heavy price?
- Are we neglecting the fundamentals of our well-being?
- Are our emotional, physical and psychological welfare being mortgaged or vanquished?
- Has our social well-being reached a tipping point?
- Above all, have we unwittingly trivialized our own well-being?

Part II

Hostages

Neither dead nor alive, the hostage is suspended by an incalculable outcome. It is not his destiny that waits for him, nor his own death, but anonymous chance, which can only seem to him something absolutely arbitrary. He is in a state of radical emergency, of virtual extermination.

—JEAN BAUDRILLARD

3

Who are Corporate Hostages?

A hostage is a person given to or held by another person, group, or organization, as a security or pledge or for ransom, release, exchange for prisoners, money, etc. A hostage could be personal, political or apolitical.

In contemporary usage, a hostage is someone who is detained by an abductor who compels others, including governments or law enforcement agencies, to act or refrain from acting in a particular way. A person who captures one or more persons by force is known as a hostage-taker.

Corporate hostages are people who work in organizations with questionable commitment, involvement and meaningfulness. They exhibit tentativeness, burnout, instability, subservience, self-centeredness and many other characteristics culminating in self-denial, unhappiness and discontentment.

Many employees are unaware of their hostage situation and are unaware of its consequences. They walk into their own incarceration as hostages since organizations do not forcibly hold them physically—unlike other hostage situations. It is more a psychological or economical captivity voluntarily created by the employees. More importantly, they become hostages to fortune (!) by pledging what they value the most, happiness. That is the true misfortune!

In any organization, do all employees enjoy their work? Seldom! They may hold positions, ranks, or be recipients of awards and rewards, and yet somehow, they live in the shadow of tentativeness, anxiety, fear of failures *and* what success might bring. It is a pity to see such 'hostages' camouflaging reality—be it in an office, at home or elsewhere, with their phony smiles and hidden stress.

The tension doesn't end there. Office parties are often full of laughter and much noise that so desperately try to hide something else. These tête-à-têtes are frequently a platform for the yes man (or woman) to please their bosses. Songs, jokes, anecdotes are all a good medium and serve to 'reinforce' this bond. Hierarchies and bosses reign supreme in this landscape. More often than not, these parties are organized to disseminate or collect information. During the OD training sessions, several executives have come up to me and confessed that their drinking habits began at such office parties, all because their superiors nudged them on. In other words, it was 'a friendly order'.

Many executives are routinely habituated to not look beyond their work/office. Anywhere else, they tend to be a fish out of water and exhibit a bleak understanding of their surroundings. Statements like 'I am married to my job' put real marriages in jeopardy.

The chairman of a family-owned ₹750-crore company once invited me as a consultant to his office. As I entered the front office, my eyes caught a statement on the wall: 'Employees in this office cannot fall sick.' I felt the office's immediate need for my services (I was called in to help with their employees' performance issues). Intrigued by the tyranny of the statement, I was curious to find out more about it.

My interaction with the executives was overwhelmingly led by my biases about this issue. Gradually, the executives revealed to me that even genuine 'sick leaves' were not encouraged. At this juncture, the chairman clarified the management's stand on this issue and justified it stating that the severity of the sickness determined the granting of leave. He went on to add, 'Unless we are strict, employees will take advantage.' While there is no disagreement on regulations, I was perturbed by the approach of the chairman. But the bigger shocker was a few employees justifying this inhumanness with this line of reasoning—that the monetary compensation offered there was better than that of competitors, and hence they felt the need to adjust. A classic setting for a hostage situation!

Hostage situations are myriad and subtly or vociferously express the corporate cultural milieu in which we live. Employees have less time for themselves or for their families. While they may have some idea about how such working styles affect their health, wealth and happiness in the long run, it is imperative for them to have a greater degree of awareness of the consequences. Balancing inner and outer peace is always difficult. Most of the time the desire for status throttles all other concerns; extravagance-driven consumerism overwhelms personal and family priorities.

Marriage is often the most common casualty of such a situation. Balancing career and marriage (not to forget, societal 'expectations') creates a potent cocktail for disaster.

I once counselled a couple who were in such a situation. In their case, the decision to have a child or not was the core issue. While both were serious about their careers, the husband preferred to have a child sooner rather than later, while the wife wanted to wait another two years to avoid hampering her professional growth. Slowly, the husband's stance shifted from a mere preference to a demand. This only strengthened the wife's decision to postpone her pregnancy. Regular conversations progressively snowballed into verbal abuse and constant fights. Compounding this were the husband's parents who persisted with their demand for a grandchild. The traditional expectations placed on a woman—bearing children and being subservient the husband, among other people—drove the wife to settle for a divorce.

While the reasons for incompatibility among couples in a marriage could be many, when they come in for a counselling session with me, prima facie it is married life vs career. Without being judgemental, a situation can be construed as straightforward or complicated depending on how one looks at it. That seems to be the reality of several married couples. Perhaps, if we were able to define one of our major concerns, we may have the necessary answers.

The complexity does not stem from our ignorance of the problem or of its resolution but perhaps because despite being aware of the resolution, the willingness to experience the consequences of that resolution preoccupies us. The fear of the unknown stops us from delving deeper into the dilemmas to seek answers. In some cases, we simply try to defend our moves: *I know what I am doing, but unless I lose something how do I gain something else?* An enlightened statement indeed, but made in the wrong context. These are the employees who willingly fall prey to the hostage syndromes discussed in the forthcoming chapter.

4

Types of Hostage Syndromes

Labelling every executive or professional as hostage and grouping them into the six hostage syndromes (see below) has never been my intention. Categorizing them under a specific syndrome does not imply they are sick or suffer from any infirmity. Many do not fall under any of these categories. These are only broad classifications for those who are still unaware but would like to understand if they are hostages or not. And if they are, which are the syndrome(s)they would manifest. The framework below invites readers to judge for themselves.

TYPES OF SYNDROMES					
Stockholm	LIMA	Risk Aversion	Greenback Cats	Blackmail	Conscience

Stockholm Syndrome

An incident in Stockholm, Sweden, served as the basis for the psychological phenomenon known as Stockholm syndrome. On 23August 1973, Kreditbank was conducting business as usual, when robbers barged in and held four bank employees hostage for a torturous five days. In an unexpected response, the employees sided with the hostage takers (robbers) during and after their ordeal and went so far as to reject efforts undertaken by the government for their rescue. The hostages exhibited their continued loyalty and even refused to testify against their captors. At one point, they even raised funds for the latter's legal expenses.[7]

In psychology, Stockholm syndrome is a term used to describe a paradoxical psychological phenomenon wherein hostages express adulation and have positive feelings for their captors. These feelings are generally considered irrational in light of the danger or risk faced by the victims, who essentially mistake the lack of flagrant abuse from their captors as an act of kindness. Studies reveal that emotional abuse blended with small acts of kindness can bond some victims to their captors even more than consistent good treatment does.

A typical example of employees suffering from Stockholm syndrome can be seen in police personnel working as orderlies (constables or junior police officers who carry out orders, perform minor tasks and run errands

[7]Adorjan, Michael, et al., 'Stockholm Syndrome as Vernacular Resource', *The Sociological Quarterly*, Vol. 53, No. 3, 2012, pp. 454–474. https://tinyurl.com/mrx2k438. Accessed on 30 May 2025.

for superior officers). The practice of deploying policemen in the camp offices of senior officers was in vogue during the British period. Gone are the British but not their system!

Today policemen stationed as security guards for their senior officers are often reduced to domestic help—an unstated job description—at the latter's residences. It has taken several years and several incidents of abuse of power for subordinate policemen to wake up to their hostage situation. In July 2018, some of them approached the Madras High Court for help to get Government of Tamil Nadu to do away with this age-old practice. Subsequently, the High Court pulled up the Home Secretary and sought an explanation regarding the practice's prevalence despite a ban in force since 1979.[8]

Even as this was taking place, several orderlies expressed (off the record) to me their willingness to be part of this practice, and wished for its continuation. Their willingness to continue doing menial jobs was astounding. From their perspective, running errands was a means to help them stay in touch with their senior officers, their family and the power associated with them. Many went so far as to praise this ill-treatment. Time and again, many senior officers have indulged in this dreadful practice, using it as a privilege over lower-ranking officials. The irony, though, of employees thriving on the treatment hasn't escaped my notice.

Private sector companies are not above this practice either. To demonstrate loyalty to upper management,

---

[8]Imranullah, Mohamed S., 'High Court frowns upon use of orderlies by police officials', *The Hindu*, 20 March 2018, https://tinyurl.com/437swdve. Accessed on 30 May 2025.

executives are more than forthcoming to carry out unhealthy practices like intra-company spying and eavesdropping, to name a few, without realizing their own hostage situation. This is a common strategy used by many C-suite leaders (executive-level managers) and/ with low-ranking employees for mutual benefit. Low-ranking staff enjoy being 'connected' to top management in lieu of unaccounted-for perks the top management offers their spy network for a clear picture of the ground reality in all departments of the organization. The result is obviously a trust deficit. When shrewd managers identify the spies, they also use them as counter-spies for their own benefit by planting misinformation to further their agendas. In that process, each one becomes a hostage to the other. Gradually, the entire organizational ecosystem becomes aware of this invisible yet divisive culture, and ends up adding to the overall ambiguity and mistrust that eventually cause maladaptive behavioural problems among all employees. Many companies still believe and consider this to be one of the best strategies in handling Industrial Relations. As a behavioural scientist, I often come across the dynamics of such a problem while handling 'Trust-Building Intervention Among Employees' in many organizations in their transactions, interplays and tensions.

While it may appear absurd to associate Stockholm syndrome with situations other than those involving kidnapping or hostage relationships, it is quite tenable to do so in hostage situations in organizations too. Research has shown that a variety of different psychological issues and forms of captivity are best explained as instances of Stockholm syndrome. Originally, Stockholm syndrome was typified as a disorder resulting from situations involving negative face-to-face contact between captors and captives. The resulting environment is one of extreme fright or terror to the victims, rendering them helpless and, over time, totally subservient to their perpetrators.

Typification helps shed light on the connection between abusive athletic and other sports coaches and consequential victimization of young athletes,[9] which can lead to Stockholm syndrome. This correlation supports the view that Stockholm syndrome relates to victimization of young athletes in a paradoxical but very real way.

Different types of victimizations have used Stockholm syndrome as a description of the paradoxical relationship between victims and their aggressors following harmful interactions or happenings. Though the feelings of loyalty and sentiment initially appear irrational and conflict with conventional wisdom, nevertheless they are present as evidence of the consequences of victimization.[10] Stockholm syndrome is a manipulation of power and trust by the captor. Thus, theoretically this syndrome relates to other forms of captivity and relationships beyond the traditional association with kidnapping. Trauma bonding, the emotional attachment victims develop toward their abusers or captors,

---

[9]Bachard, Charles, and Niki Djak, 'Stockholm Syndrome in Athletics: A Paradox', *Children Australia*, Vol. 43, No. 3, September 2018, pp. 175–180, https://tinyurl.com/2zan634u. Accessed on 30 May 2025.

[10]Cantor, Chris, and John Price, 'Traumatic Entrapment, Appeasement and Complex Post-Traumatic Stress Disorder: Evolutionary Perspectives of Hostage Reactions, Domestic Abuse and the Stockholm Syndrome', *Australian & New Zealand Journal of Psychiatry*, Vol. 41, No. 5, 2007, pp. 377–384. https://tinyurl.com/4swtrnkv. Accessed on 30 May 2025.

has been repeatedly observed in victims of interpersonal crimes.[11] In athletics, the victimization of young athletes results in Stockholm syndrome, affecting them deeply.

Lima Syndrome

In Lima syndrome, abductors/hostage-takers develop sympathy for their hostages, unlike Stockholm syndrome, where the abductees are sympathetic towards their captors. The more surprising and paradoxical element of Lima syndrome is that the captors often behave as if they never held the victim(s) hostage in the first place. In many cases, they turned out to be caregivers who provided comfort and solace to their hostages. They also tend to get emotionally involved and connected to their victims and have their feelings reciprocated as well. From the behaviour of the captors towards their hostages, what has been frequently observed is that the former—

- Indulge in conversation
- Assure their victims of safe release
- Provide their victims some freedom to move around
- Do not indulge in physical abuse
- Often share personal details like their desire and goals with their victims

An incident in Lima, Peru, gave this syndrome its moniker. In 1996, fourteen members of the revolutionary group

---

[11]Bilali, Klejdis, Emily D. Walker, and Joan A. Reid, 'Trauma Bonding and Hostage-Taking/Kidnapping', *Wiley*, 5 July 2024, pp. 99–119, https://tinyurl.com/68sxbuyt. Accessed on 30 May 2025.

Movimiento Revolucionario Túpac Amaru (MRTA) took hundreds of people hostage while they were attending a party hosted at the Japanese Ambassador's official residence. With the intervention of the Peruvian military, the embassy was secured and the hostages released. During the storming of the embassy by the military, some abductors lost their lives. However, as reported by the media, there was appreciation for the abductors mainly about how they set female hostages free within a relatively short period of time. Ironically, despite the abductors' initial plan to kill all the hostages,[12] [13] their final sympathy for their victims was on full display.

The principle drawn from the above syndrome is how perpetrators fall in love with their victims. In a corporate scenario, we may have come across cases where the management prefers/likes certain people and entices them to take on more work and they go on to become the management's favourites. They are showered with special perks openly or discreetly. Slowly the management becomes dependent on these favourites. Ironically, both become hostages knowingly or unknowingly at each other's hands.

The work culture in India is still deeply entrenched in the colonial mindset. An employee leaving office before their boss, not putting in overtime (paid or unpaid)

---

[12]Lama, Abraham, 'PERU: Tale of a Kidnapping—from Stockholm to Lima Syndrome', *Inter Press Service*, 10 July 1996, https://tinyurl.com/45k5kce5. Accessed on 30 May 2025.

[13]Kim, Yoshiharu, 'Current Perspectives on Clinical Studies of PTSD in Japan', *PTSD: Brain Mechanisms and Clinical Implications*, Kato, N., M. Kawata, and R.K. Pitman (eds.), *Springer-Verlag*, 2006, p. 149.

irrespective of the work demands is a classic example of a worker 'without a positive attitude'. On the contrary, those who leave office after their bosses are considered good employees even though they may not be the most efficient ones. Among them are those who fear for their jobs, and therefore cannot afford to confront their bosses despite their suffering. This fear works to the advantage of their bosses. It encourages them to prey on the fears of employees who are non-confrontational in the long run and to retain them as hostages.

Having worked and consulted in various corporates over four decades, I have personal experience of how a slave system operates covertly in many organizations, demanding subordinates to stay put in the office till the bosses leave. I was once reprimanded for leaving office on time despite completing my work for the day. What mattered was not the quality of work done but the extra time you spend massaging the ego of bosses, or to 'show' what a serious worker you are.

Many Baby Boomers and Gen Xers are accustomed to this culture that prevailed back then. Surprisingly, they equated this behaviour with showing loyalty to the company. This expectation has somewhat percolated down to the next generation, who still believes the above 'virtue' needs to be cultivated. Senior managers still complain to me that Millennials and Gen Zers are bereft of this virtue and they want to leave office on the dot of time. The former considers the attitude of the latter as indiscipline and indicative of a lack of focus on their job. Superiors often demand that subordinates be subservient to their oppressive behaviour. Meritorious employees perhaps avoid becoming hostage to this situation, but mediocre employees may resort to this to compensate for their professional incompetencies.

In 1990, a *Fortune* cover story titled 'Why "Grade A" Executives get an "F" as parents?' observed that children of successful executives are more likely to go through a range of emotional and health problems than children of 'less successful' parents.[14] Traditional managements cultivate the rift between work and family, sometimes consciously. The unwritten threat is if you want to climb the professional ladder, you must be ready to sacrifice your family time—which may lead to a conflict between work and family.[15] Covid has taught many to redefine their lives by highlighting the importance of health, family and congeniality, rather than the mindless pursuit of money.

Despite Indian labour laws specifying forty-eight hours work time a week, overtly or covertly employees are coerced to work well beyond their regular office hours. Maintaining work-life balance for employees means little to many organizations, especially owner-driven companies.

While the debate on this subject still rages on in formal set-ups and social media, top business leader N.R. Narayana Murthy of Infosys expected employees to work seventy hours a week to enhance productivity, while S.N. Subrahmanyan, Chairman, Larsen & Toubro, wanted employees to work ninety hours a week. To make matters worse, Mr Subrahmanyan added: 'I regret I am not able to

---

[14]O'Reilly, Brian, 'Why Grade "A" Executives Get an "F" as Parents', *Fortune*, 1 January 1990.

[15]Senge, Peter M., 'Chapter 16: Ending the War Between Work and Family', *The Fifth Discipline: The Art and Practice of the Learning Organization*, Doubleday Currency,1990, New York, p. 306.

make you to work on Sundays.' [...] 'What do you do sitting at home? How long can you stare at your wife? How long can the wife stare at the husband?' Few supported these business leaders' views.

The Indian culture of overworking employees is a growing concern and poses many challenges to organizations, especially with the imminent increase in the presence of Gen Z in the workforce.

An 'Indeed' survey found that '88% of Indian employees are contacted by their employers outside of regular working hours, with 85% stating that communication continues even during public holidays or sick leave. Among these workers, 79% expressed concerns that not responding after office hours could affect their career progression and promotion and damaged reputations.'[16] Gen Z is not entering the workforce for want of their basic and safety needs which are well taken care of by their parents. Their expectations are centred predominantly around peer acceptance and self-esteem. With a lack of understanding of their needs, the vicious cycle of complaining about the non-adaptability and non-alignment of the forthcoming generation is bound to repeat itself.

Risk Aversion

Risk aversion can be classified as the tendency of some people to reduce the possibility of uncertainty or to avoid it. Situations where people work towards a more predictable

---

[16]*ET Online,* 'Is 90 Hours a Week Legal? Here's What Indian Labour Laws Say about 'Working Overtime', *The Economic Times,* 20 January 2025, https://tinyurl.com/3jfmxaen. Accessed on 30 May 2025.

but lower payoff rather than a higher, unknown payoff would also come under this syndrome. Let's take the example of a risk-averse investor. Such a person may choose to put money in a bank account with a low but guaranteed rate of interest, rather than in a stock which may have higher expected returns but also runs the risk of dropping in value.

It is not uncommon to see such behaviour among employees. Risk averse employee do not upset the status quo by deviating from standard procedures. Their tendency to see goals as opportunities to maintain the status quo ensures things keep running smoothly. Higgins calls this 'prevention focus.'[17] This is associated with a robust aversion to being wide-eyed and optimistic, taking chances and making mistakes.

Risk averters may not be content with their work, power or perks. However, this attitude holds them hostage as it may deter their creativity, intuitiveness and growth which are not their priorities. They become insensitive to forecasting or estimating possible alternatives while making decisions in critical situations.

Risk averters come in many forms and settings. Let's take an example of sales executives. Visualize sales executives in the process of fixing their annual sales targets. They set their target low even though they are aware that fixing a higher target means more incentives. Despite being aware of a lower incentive opportunity, the willingness to forgo

---

[17]Higgins, E. Tory, 'Promotion and Prevention: Regulatory Focus as A Motivational Principle', *Advances in Experimental Social Psychology*, Vol. 30, 1998, pp. 1–46, https://tinyurl.com/5c6phu79. Accessed on 6 May2025.

higher aspirations is a classic attribute of a risk averter. Risk averters consider this optimal target setting will ensure their performance with ease, rather than risking a failure to achieve a much higher target that may expose them to disapproval from their superiors. This decision is a trade-off between the benefits and costs of extra effort and the choice risk averters make to avoid an uncertain outcome of the demands made on them. Many consider this a safe bet rather than exploring new paths, which may bring out their true potential.

They consider stability as the key for their survival as they doubt their competencies and outcome. The trees are more important for them than the forests as they lack in vision. Their psychological underpinnings play *devil's advocacy* to themselves on why things will not go successfully.

Risk takers, on the other hand, are often deemed more successful than 'wise' people who are risk averse. Risk takers tend to seize the opportunity and exhibit their competencies to succeed in their assignment with strategies, be it operational, marketing or inventing new products. Their optimistic attitude doesn't deter them taking risks. While the risks they take seem irrational, even unnecessary, to risk-averse people, their decisions are based on sound logic, keeping in mind the vital cause-and-effect factor. They work towards experiential learning rather than achieving success. They question the status quo and tend to think *out of the box.*

To my surprise, many organizations and their executives advocate change as a key driver for the organization's growth but shun risk takers in practice. In addition, their tendency to punish risk takers for their failed attempt in open forums discourages others from thinking out of the box.

Karen Firestone, the author of the book titled *Even the Odds: Sensible Risk-Taking in Business, Investing, and Life* (2016), deals with risks every day. She is the president and CEO of Aureus Asset Management, an investment firm that manages the assets of companies and individuals. While researching her book, she spoke to many people about the risks they take in their own lives and came to an interesting conclusion. Oftentimes, the safest path is really the riskiest one. Firestone finds that many of the seemingly safe decisions we make bet on one unrealistic condition: that nothing in the circumstances will ever change. She says, 'I've come to the conclusion that although most of us consider ourselves risk averse, what we consider safe behavior often contains much more uncertainty than we suspect.'[18]

Blackmail

Possibly the most easily identifiable hostage syndrome is blackmail. Any person who threatens others to part with something in lieu of something tangible or intangible can be defined as a blackmailer. While we may have experienced situations involving blackmailers in our personal lives, they are very much part of the corporate world. Corporate

---

[18]Firestone, Karen, 'Why That Risky Career Move Could Be a Safer Bet than You Think', *Harvard Business Review*, 11 March 2016, https://tinyurl.com/4vwtzed8. Accessed on 6 May 2025.

blackmailers often function covertly and overtly. Employers, employees, management—anyone can fit this mould. Normally, an individual or entity who blackmails would have sensitive and/or damaging information or matter on the blackmailed. They would threaten to come forward with the same unless the blackmailed comply with their demands.

Instances of blackmail occur frequently during discontinuity of employment. Blackmailing within an organization can be critical, causing serious problems ranging from ruining an individual's career prospects to pushing the company into financial distress.

An employee once reached out to me regarding a problem he and some colleagues were facing in their organization. They had been working as software engineers in a large company. Due to personal and professional reasons, they had accepted new positions at a smaller software firm. As professional courtesy, they provided their current employer with two months' notice—double the required one-month notice period.

Despite consistently receiving above-average performance reviews and earning promotions during their tenure, they were informed after one month that if they did not extend their departure date, their exit would be considered as leaving 'on bad terms'. This was implied subtly, yet unmistakably.

With only three weeks remaining for their planned departure, they were reluctant to escalate the matter to Human Resources, fearing that might worsen the situation. Still, the pressure and unethical implications of the management's request were deeply concerning. Being in an 'at-will' employment state, they were aware that the company had no legal grounds to force them to stay. However, what troubled them most was the potential impact on future references. Having spent most of their career with this employer, they were understandably concerned about how this might affect their professional reputation and future opportunities. The individual who had got in touch with me wondered if others had ever faced a similar situation and how they had navigated it.

The answer is 'yes'. Most employees' grievances are often centred around quitting. It doesn't matter if they had a pleasant experience while working or otherwise. I have seen and heard firsthand about the sudden hostile attitude that managers develop toward employees who are quitting. The threat of blackmail will either be subtle or loud depending on the behaviour of the quitter.

While so-called 'professional' companies indulge in such unethical practices, much is to be said about absolutely 'unprofessional' companies that demand the prospective employee's educational certificate as a bond. Although this blackmailing phenomenon by employers is predominant in India, today's technology has given rise to new methods where employees steal significant employer data or indulge in hacking. The only difference here is that the data serves to hold the employer hostage.

A perfect example of this would be the 'Paytm Extortion Case'. The founder of India's largest e-wallet company was allegedly threatened by his personal secretary of many years. Her ten-year stint in Paytm saw her rise from the ranks of a secretary to head of corporate communications in the company. Her plan to extort ₹20 crore from her boss was put into motion by stealing the founder's personal data from his laptop, phones and office desktop. She, along with her husband and another colleague, was accused of these charges. The law enforcement was obliged to reckon that this was purely a case of personal data theft and they were arrested.[19]

Greenback Cats

Greenback Cats are a species of fundamentalists who live in a world of wealth. Their senses are auto-tuned and animated to pick up signals both individually and collectively when they see, hear, touch, smell or taste money. No other socially relevant demand or motivation attracts them. Their obsessive loyalty is reserved for money, and oftentimes they are willing to relinquish other physical and psychological needs only to amass wealth.

The word Greenback first appeared in American English during the American Civil War in 1862, when officials in Washington felt the need for more financial resources than others. Although state banks circulated paper money, the federal government restricted it to coins only. When coins started disappearing, the American government decided to issue paper money. To prevent counterfeits, a special patented green-coloured ink was used instead of the usual black. Due to this distinctive colour, union soldiers began referring to this paper currency as 'greenbacks'.

---

[19]'Paytm extortion case: How Paytm's Vijay Shekhar Sharma was blackmailed by his personal secretary', *Business Today*, 24 October 2018, https://tinyurl.com/y387pv7v. Accessed on 6 May 2025.

Greenback syndrome can be associated with greediness and is marked by an eager and often selfish desire for material possessions. Manfred F.R. Kets De Vries, a clinical professor of leadership and organizational change, writes: 'What I have learned from experience dealing with executives that suffer from the greed syndrome is that it is usually the foolish decisions borne out of greed that eventually prompts them to realize their mistakes. Often setbacks, such as health issues or serious interpersonal problems, propel them to confront their addiction to greed.'[20]

Greed and excess are hallmarks of many executives. These characteristics cut across most human endeavours and go back as long as our species has been on earth. Throughout humankind's history, greed has had a mixed press. On the one hand, it has been hailed as the motor of economic growth and human progress, on the other, uncontrolled greed has been seen as the cause of much misery, as recent economic history has very dramatically demonstrated. Despite these examples, our culture continues to place a premium on materialism and, by extension, greed.

While the greedy continue to look for limitless money, which may buy them more than they require, the 'needy' generally tend to set a limit for their monetary horizon. Money is often a synonym for success. Every greedy action carries a certain level of aggression, maybe even unethical

---

[20]De Vries, Manfred F.R. Kets, 'Seven Signs of the Greed Syndrome', *INSEAD Knowledge*, INSEAD, https://tinyurl.com/c6c2bekw. Accessed on 6 May 2025.

choices and in some cases even non-monetary losses.

Looking at scams in India or in other parts of the world—the result is always the same. Looting! It is about looting either the government's or the common people's money. High-profile companies or business tycoons—from Enron, Tyco and Satyam Computers to Nirav Modi, Mehul Choksi and Vijay Mallya, among countless others—have been in the news for all the wrong reasons, forever showcasing their huge haul (public money) while conniving with the very people elected to power to safeguard the public's interest. These scams were not initiated by the owners of the company alone; these were facilitated and executed by the CEOs, CFOs and other senior managers and leaders of these companies. Ultimately, people who are consumed by the desire to acquire others' money (unethically) will end up as hostages or prisoners themselves of their own greed.

Hostage by Conscience

A syndrome that is fundamentally different in principle and evolution is 'Hostage by Conscience'. In psychology, conscience refers to our intuitive feeling as a compass that guides us to carry out our activities, be it right or wrong. It is our 'voice within' that justifies our actions.

People who claim *'I know what I am doing'* and/or *'I have no other choice'* qualify for this syndrome. They may belong to any one or multiple combinations of the previous five syndromes. The key distinction of hostages emerging from this syndrome is that they are better informed and aware of the pros and cons of the choices they make. They are armed with a conscious understanding of the consequences they may face due to their decisions and walk into traps set up by themselves, or they work within the limited choices the world offers them for survival.

I know what I am doing

The longevity of a person in a company and this syndrome are mutually inclusive. Employees who stay on in a company for several years, albeit without reasonable growth, usually do not dare to seek a job elsewhere. The fear of treading in another unknown company, and the unthreatening climate in the existing company, often encourages them to stay where they are.

This process usually starts with the employees getting more than they offer in the bargain. Such employees often know exactly why they stay in a company and what they do and can do. People with moderate self-esteem, risk averters, power and status chasers, and underdogs fit in this category. People in this category are generally intelligent and have the potential, but tend to harbour self-doubt and allow it to become a key hindrance in their career advancement.

A few years ago, an MBA from a top management institute in India, who had been working in a medium-sized manufacturing company as Head of Operations for more than twelve years, met me for professional advice during a training workshop with the intent of learning how to handle stress. His pressure arose out of discontentment and unhappiness when compared with his batchmates who held positions in upper management (Chairman, CEO, COO, etc). Upon probing why he did not switch jobs and look for better positions, he stated, 'I know why I am here. I don't blame my management as they have always been understanding.' He continued to narrate how he has always been respected in the present company and went on to admit, 'I think I fear handling bigger responsibilities and the position that comes with that, but it still haunts me when I meet my batchmates.' Even before ending the conversation, he was quick to say he knew the answer to his problems. True! People avoid taking on bigger responsibilities despite the elevation in their position mainly due to fear of failure or fear of the next challenge success might bring.

Fear of success

Though fear of failure and fear of success seem to be opposites, the psychological underpinning is the same: self-doubt. To differentiate the two more precisely, fear of failure arises due to worry over what others think of one's performance, whereas fear of success stems from one's internal anxiety of unknown responsibilities and their consequences. I remember a colleague with twenty years of experience, heading the finance department in his organization, was offered the chance to head an upcoming SBU (strategic business unit), which he declined. The chairman of my company requested that I motivate him to take up the position. While acknowledging the recognition of his competencies to lead the unit, his anxiety propelled by his self-doubt withheld him. He explained that though he was happy with the recognition, he felt that he was not ready for the new role and not sure about the trade-off and the benefits of the switch. In short, he was not ready to let himself down. It was not the elevation to the position itself that he feared; the potential price of future success bothered him.

Increased responsibilities and their fulfilment may deter people's growth. Their cognitive and emotional brain can eclipse their true potential and convince them and others of their unpreparedness. This is an act of self-sabotage that hinders one's growth.

I have no other choice

In December 2019, when the first case of Covid-19 was reported from Wuhan, China, it didn't garner much attention. But the contagious disease severely impacted the world, drastically changing employment conditions, financial security, and overall well-being of people and of their families. The widespread coronavirus pushed many organizations, especially SMEs, to slow down, scale back or fold up operations. Average performers in various industries were mostly afflicted with anxiety disorders, thanks to the heightened prospect of losing their jobs. They overlooked the criticality of balancing family and life. Many had to focus on extended working hours to achieve targets to retain their jobs. Many employees said that they left their homes without any guarantee of returning. The challenges emerging from the pandemic gave rise to a 'Catch 22' hostage situation. You need money, go to work; if you go to work, you may die! People felt they had been left without a choice.

To contain this perilous situation and to safeguard people and their organizations from the dreaded disease, organizations globally came out with a clever formula called 'Work from Home' (WFH). The very suggestion would hold different meanings pre-Covid. It was encouraged during Covid-19. Though the option of WFH initially provided a breather to all, soon a few began to feel suffocated. Subsequently, a substantial chunk of employees started comparing their situation with house arrest. This hostage situation had multiple effects on people—physically, mentally and economically, not just during Covid, but in the post-Covid era too despite being a choice made by one's own conscience.

It was a great lesson for all types of hostages mentioned earlier. People with Stockholm syndrome and Lima syndrome were able to understand how they manipulated others and how they were manipulated by others. Blackmailers might have understood their shoddy acts carried no value when the whole world was reeling under uncertainty. Risk averters discerned that they had encountered a great risk in their lives. Greenback Cats realized their misplaced priority of just chasing money.

Indeed, clarity dawned on many—retrospectively though—that they need to accept their vulnerabilities and upskill their competencies. A shift in their attitude from *'I know what I am doing is right'* to *'I need to review what I am doing'* registered in the minds of a few in their learning curve.

Sadly, the lessons learnt from Covid seem to have been forgotten, rather than being permanently lodged in everyone's lives, including the lives of professionals. I recognize now that many good performers are embracing the syndrome of 'choice by one's own conscience'. Maybe the essence of the word 'contentment' is misinterpreted here.

Recap		
Syndrome	**Theme**	**Organizational Perspectives**
STOCKHOLM	Hostages tend to harbour and express positive feelings towards their captors.	Loyalty towards management remains high, while employees may psychologically, not physically, be held hostage.
LIMA	Captivators express sympathy towards their hostages.	The management/superiors may show partiality and/or sympathy towards certain employees whom they 'hold hostage'.
RISK AVERSION	Hostages resign themselves to a life of mediocrity without utilizing their optimum capability.	The fear of treading unknown paths forces employees to maintain their status quo. Treading on tried and tested ground is the safest option for them.

BLACKMAIL	Hostages aim to achieve their goals by threatening others.	Employees often possess vital information on product secrets, processes and the business itself, and threaten to destabilize the company for their own benefit.
GREENBACK CATS	Hostages are bound only by money and material gains which are often the only motivators in their lives.	The willingness to relinquish one's personal, social and psychological needs in order to amass wealth is the only goal for these employees.
HOSTAGE BY CONSCIENCE	Hostages have a 'know it all here' confidence about themselves and operate in a limited environment, shunning other choices.	Hostages are aware of their vulnerabilities and their limited choices to want to continue in their present employment. They may also exhibit a combination of characteristics of other syndromes.

Part III

Concerns and Conundrums

One of the basic rules of the universe is that nothing is perfect. Perfection simply doesn't exist... Without imperfection, neither you nor I would exist.

—STEPHEN HAWKING

5

Quick Fixes and Shortcuts

A myriad of 'quick fixes' are scattered around us as intoxicating agents to our mind and body. These pills often act as formulae for quick results. These 'quick fix' pills are taken without bitterness, regardless of the ensuing results.

Shortcuts are not to be equated with finding alternative methods or deviating from the prescribed routes. All sprinters would have a wealth of experience in falling down, stumbling, contracted muscles and other hurdles while they were on track. What shortcuts could they have taken to win? If so, would they have been successful in the long run? There are quite a few instances when Olympians were stripped of their medals on doping/drug charges. Even at their peak, using shortcuts to reach the end earned them nothing but notoriety.

Although India is an economically developing nation, the education system is lagging behind by several years. Are we not often taught inorganic theories that enable us to achieve success, albeit without realizing why we are the way we are? Quality education is traditionally mortgaged to grades (marks), which somehow become the *sine qua non* of being able to pursue higher education, and acts as a gateway for admissions in universities/colleges. In return, many higher educational facilities compromise on quality and produce fragile and vulnerable graduates for the workforce. This infectious disease has now become chronic in our educational landscape.

A related issue that stems from people's tendency to constantly look for quick fixes and shortcuts is that they seldom make an effort to find out who they are. They are either unaware of the importance of knowing themselves or lessen the significance of self-realization through their callous attitude. They aspire to be who they want to be without ever finding out who they truly are! This is akin to sowing seeds without understanding the soil. While plants grow and bloom by their very nature, without any understanding of the soil, they may fail to flourish.

South and Southeast Asian countries have long believed, preached and practised the spiritual way of life. In recent years, there has been a visible shift from this 'system'. The misconceived celebrations of a successful few tend to influence many others, who wait excitedly for their turn. However, in their quest for belongings, most end up losing their sense of belonging.

During job interviews, recruiters love to say, 'Tell me something about yourself" or 'Describe yourself'. Most of the time, these questions elicit interesting responses. There have been occasions when I have had my questions met with a passive response or surprise coated with bewilderment. *How can I talk about myself?* Probing further often revealed their belief that talking about oneself is inappropriate.

Disclosure on the self has been construed as negative and akin to blowing one's own trumpet. Many conclude that a simple bio data suffices for sharing information about oneself. Growth without knowing oneself can stunt life, the rest of the circumstances notwithstanding.

The thirst for earning degrees, certificates and promotions has created a culture where people want to do everything as quickly as possible. They presume that holding multiple degrees and certificates is more valuable than their actual competence in those domains and the quality of their work. They do not enjoy going through the relevant processes anymore. To fulfil this need, they start to look for shortcuts and strategies that save them time and energy. Many might have been shocked to read about PhD theses being sold for thirty thousand rupees in Delhi[21] or about the arrest of an IAS aspirant for impersonating his friend in another major government exam for a fee of ₹1 lakh[22].

I once had the misfortune of witnessing civil services aspirants employing these shortcuts, which sadly are taught by the same coaching centres that charge exorbitant fees to help prepare these aspirants for the competitive exams. It is indeed sad to watch how these coaching academies and students spend time devising such devious strategies. Officers who one day are supposed to help effect political,

---

[21]Lidhoo, Prerna, 'Up for Grabs: PhD Thesis Available for Rs 30K in South Delhi Markets', *Hindustan Times*, 30 March 2016, https://tinyurl.com/3vnx354e. Accessed on 2 June 2025.

[22]*Indo-Asian News Service*, 'IAS Aspirant Held for Impersonation', *NDTV*, 12 July 2011, https://tinyurl.com/yvmcx6de. Accessed on 2 June 2025.

socioeconomic changes are taught to believe that the end is more important than the means.

Civil service coaching centres are expected to shape aspirants holistically—nurturing ethics, integrity and professionalism, alongside preparing them for success in the selection process. Yet, the very language of their advertisements, with their focus on 'cracking' exams and interviews, reveals much about their real priorities. The mushrooming of these centres as a thriving industry has fostered a competitive edge among them, prompting many to resort to questionable practices. These include inflated claims of success rate, making lofty promises of guaranteed selection, etc.[23] [24]

As for the aspirants, many arrive in metropolitan cities such as Delhi and Chennai, treating the coaching stint as a transitional phase while they look for employment—or, in the case of some women candidates—as a way to delay impending matrimony. Some coaching centres, whose primary business is to prepare civil services hopefuls, quietly steer students unlikely to succeed in the central services towards state-level exams. In such cases, selection is often 'guaranteed' for a price—an understanding that remains, for the most part, unspoken.

---

[23]Ministry of Consumer Affairs, Food & Public Distribution, 'CCPA Imposes Penalties on Coaching Institutes for Misleading Advertisements Regarding UPSC CSE Results', *Press Information Bureau*, 26 December 2024, https://tinyurl.com/42hznhed. Accessed on 2 June 2025.

[24]Bhutani, Chetan, 'Unacademy, Byju's IAS, Drishti IAS among 20 Coaching Institutes under Scanner for Misleading Claims: Sources', *Business Today*, 23 October 2023, https://tinyurl.com/4re42zu2. Accessed on 2 June 2025.

Many prefer shortcuts as a legitimate strategy, notwithstanding the possible unfavourable results in the long run. People often engage in shortcuts due to one of the following reasons:

- Feeling of helplessness
- Fear of facing challenges
- Dubious role models
- Lack of willingness to learn

Feeling of helplessness

Helplessness often arises out of unjustified empirical data or past undemonstrated behaviour. It is simply instilling an untested notion. When the cognitive faculty has not been initiated, it leads to frustration that pushes us to a state of helplessness. Clinical psychologists posit helplessness and hopelessness as typical symptoms of depressive disorders. Traits of vulnerability and risk aversion reinforce this situation. The cognitive theory of depression put forth by A.T. Beck defines 'hopelessness as negative expectancies concerning the future and helplessness unrealistically belittle concepts of one's own capabilities.'

Beck considers such a negative view of the self and the future as a central element of the 'cognitive triad' that consists of negative attitudes toward the self, the future and the environment. According to this theory, the cognitive triad plays a specific aetiological role in depression. The basic hypothesis is that a cognitive disturbance precedes the affective change and is responsible for its maintenance. Before the onset of dysphoria and depression, the affected person is considered to misinterpret reality through a negative cognitive screen.[25]

The fundamental lack of awareness of one's capabilities promotes misinterpretation of the reality of the self and the situation. Those who have lost touch with themselves are detached from their souls and are not attuned to heed their inner voice. Shunning one's inner voice often means being less acquainted with one's own potencies and inherent strengths that can otherwise be displayed, but that is deeply buried, even dormant, due to lack of awareness.

Continued practice of this apathy towards the self makes people excessively dependent. Unexplored potencies remain hidden since they are neither tested nor challenged. Eventually, people form a notion of helplessness and are forced to adapt to their environment at the cost of their self-esteem. You may have come across many such people in the workplace. Ironically, executives misconstrue this adaptation as the best way to climb the corporate ladder. Unfortunately, by this point, they have already tamed themselves to the company's culture and unwittingly become a 'Trojan Horse' to the company, oblivious of their involvement as soldiers for the organization's victory—a point that may be better illustrated with a short story.

▪

[25]Henkel, V., P. Bussfeld, H.J. Möller, and U. Hegerl, 'Cognitive-Behavioural Theories of Helplessness/Hopelessness: Valid Models of Depression?', *European Archives of Psychiatry and Clinical Neuroscience*, Vol. 252, No. 5, October 2002, pp. 240–49, https://tinyurl.com/3fk5vc7z. Accessed on 6 May 2025.

Five Monkeys and a Banana

A medical experiment was undertaken in which five monkeys were placed together in a room with a banana hanging high above from a rope, beyond their reach. A ladder was placed in the room that would enable the monkeys to reach the banana. Whenever one of the monkeys attempted to climb it and reach for the banana, all the monkeys were sprayed with freezing cold water.

After a few attempts, all the monkeys learned the association between reaching for the banana and the collective punishment of being sprayed with freezing water. There was no longer any need for the freezing water punishment, as they were conditioned not to attempt to reach for the banana.

The researcher then replaced one of the five monkeys with a new one. The new monkey, not yet aware of the cold-water treatment, tried to reach for the banana. Soon the other four monkeys attacked it repeatedly, until it gave up on its attempts to reach the banana. One by one, the monkeys who were initially part of the experiment were replaced with a new monkey. With the introduction of each new monkey, the other monkeys would attack the new entrant until they quit trying to reach for the banana.

Eventually, the room was filled with five new monkeys who had no experience of the cold-water treatment. The researcher then introduced an additional new monkey to the room. When this monkey tried to reach for the banana, the other five monkeys attacked it. This practice continued for some time and then ceased. The newer monkeys who were enlisted later were neither exposed to the cold-water treatment nor group punishment. However, along the way they learnt that reaching for the banana was not allowed.

▪

The story exemplifies that the culture that is built over time eventually becomes the guiding principle without any knowledge of its purpose. People who are distant from their own selves and who prefer not to challenge existing systems and rules would find this type of atmosphere very conducive. Most newcomers, however, frown upon the current culture, oblivious of the management's unwritten cultural coding. They may end up undergoing the monkey experiment and creating an unquestioning and malleable attitude.

Fear of Facing Challenges

Fear can broadly be defined as 'a rational physiological response to a clearly perceived or anticipated external danger that prompts an individual to flee or attack in self-defence.'[26] The Oxford Dictionary says that fear is an unpleasant emotion caused by the threat of danger. Another dimension of fear is that it can be rational as well as irrational. The moot point here is our misunderstanding of fear and its consequences. Allow me to explain.

Imagine you are walking in a village overrun by trees and vegetation. It is a refreshing experience away from the

---

[26]Lewis, Michael, Jeannette M. Haviland-Jones, and Lisa Feldman Barrett (eds.), *Handbook of Emotions*. 3rd ed., Guilford Press, New York, 2008, pp. 294, 666.

concrete jungles that you negotiate in a modern city. While you are being buffeted by a gentle breeze and you allow yourself to take in all the greenery, you find a snake in front of you. You aren't sure if it is poisonous or not. It waits for you like a host would. Since you don't know how to relate to snakes or to this situation, you run amok and escape. Even after you have reached the main road, you turn back to ensure the snake has not followed you. It doesn't help that this fleeting feeling crops up whenever you are near a bush or taking a walk in a heavily wooded area.

Let's look at the psychological underpinnings of this phenomenon. When you see yourself standing in front of a snake, in the thick woods, you may develop a rational reaction of fleeing. Objectively you sense an external danger and hence the accompaniment of fear. Yet, somehow you have the same feeling of fear, whenever you cross a wooded area or a bush even when there is no danger of snakes. This experience would firmly fit into Pavlov's classical conditioning theory.[27] Your mind has been conditioned, and an association has already been made, pairing any bush/wooded area with snakes.

Even in the absence of a potent stimulus (snakes), a neutral stimulus (bushes) can elicit the same response of wanting to flee. When there is no actual external danger,

---

[27]Ivan Pavlov studied the behaviour of dogs and developed a theory of classical conditioning, which explains how people associate two stimuli in their minds and react to one of them as though it were the other. Sanvictores, Terrence, Navid Mahabadi, and Chaudhry I. Rehman, 'Classical Conditioning,' *National Library of Medicine*, updated 5 September 2024, https://tinyurl.com/2sdk6wdv. Accessed on 6 May 2025.

the consequent feeling becomes irrational.

The certainty of events causes fear; the uncertainty of events causes anxiety. Children experiencing fear during and around their exams is not fear; it is anxiety. This anxiety gradually becomes a disorder due to negligence or ineffective handling and poses a potential harm throughout their lives.

Are we not constantly and consistently frightened of many things in our daily life? This disorder shows up at our workplace too, and could be triggered during meetings with superiors or for a business review, presentations, and/or public meetings. People tend to turn down transfers, promotions and greater responsibilities all due to anxiety. Although life-threatening symptoms do not show up in our normal workplace, people often struggle with low self-esteem when faced with everyday challenges. In my experience, mediocrity stands out and is eventually exposed in the long run. The absence of an appropriate understanding of the difference between fear and anxiety has ruined the human race in many ways.

In the late nineties I joined as Head of Corporate HR in one of India's leading business conglomerates. A pan-India operation, they had more than twenty companies of varied businesses employing more than fifty thousand people. The managerial staff accounted for about fifteen per cent of the total employee count.

I was heading a key department of the company, which had eight units, with about six thousand employees. This company was known for its employee-centric approach and its robust financial accountability systems. The employees never doubted for a second that their jobs would ever be at stake in this fifty-year-old company. They strongly believed in the motto 'Hired till you are retired'. One of the prime cultures prevalent within this company was 'recognizing the employee's loyalty over performance'. Dispensing with the services of the management for poor performance was never a practice even though ostensibly it was the company's prerogative.

Responding to emerging global economic challenges back then, this company too jumped on the bandwagon and was eager to bring about changes involving business process, reengineering and lean management structure. As a precursor, it roped in the help of an external consultancy to study, diagnose, and deliver its suggestions for improvement. The first salvo from the consultancy was to cut down ten per cent of the existing management staff.

Before this operation, the HR department initiated close meetings with poor performers, but who were loyal to the company, and wanted to sensitize them about their performance and accountability. Those who paid no heed to the HR department's efforts were the only ones slated to be sent out as an outcome of the consultancy's reengineering plan. It was an unhappy phase for me when these hundred-odd employees shook hands with HR upon their termination. They resigned due to their inability to change, save for a few who wanted time to improve. None among the hundred could believe what was happening. Our relocation efforts to other companies through recruitment agencies failed too, as they were considered high on the list of 'skill shortage'. Their woes and despair lingered on for long. Several years after this incident, when I met a few of them, I was convinced that they had finally understood the meaning of 'loyalty' and its effects, albeit at a huge personal cost.

Thus, it is simple: meritocracy can never be defeated by mediocrity or loyalty alone in the long run. Shortcuts that involve being loyal or subservient only tend to result in a complete derailment of one's career.

Dubious Role Models

I once came across two college students loudly debating about their futures in the middle of a college canteen. One of them wanted to discontinue his studies and become a politician. He justified to his friend how this venture could bring him and his family great fortune. I found his stance on the topic somewhat amusing and listened further. What dumbfounded me was *not what he wanted to be,* but *how he wanted to be that!* He spoke about his uncle, who was a politician and had amassed huge amounts of wealth in a relatively short period. Furthermore, his uncle was tipped to become a minister soon. At this point, his friend confronted him by stating how corrupt politicians would end up in jail one day and advised him against choosing this as a career. The friend's concern was met with disdain when the aspiring politician replied that going to jail was part of that profession.

That dialogue sounded straight out of a cheesy movie. After listening to their conversation, I wasn't sure whether he was joking or seriously proposing to become a politician. However, the thought I was left with was the emergence of dubious role models, and admirers aspiring to follow in their footsteps. In India, and in all probability in other countries too, many criminals have gone on to become ministers who flaunt their wealth, power and fame, and in turn become role models for the country's youth.

People who do not know themselves and who believe in the overt importance of the self without adequate rationale tend to be disastrous role models setting off a chain of disastrous experiences. A few corporate honchos take their cue from these politicians and build their empire, neglecting basic personal and social ethics in their corporate kingdom. It is an unfortunate paradox that these corporate leaders, too, will become role models for executives and entrepreneurs.

The Satyam Computers ruination has hardly been wiped from the memories of many Indians and the larger corporate set-up. A once successful IT giant, to attract investments, its chairman falsely boosted its revenue by 1.5 billion dollars, fudging revenues, margins and cash balances. Eight employees, along with the chairman, were found guilty of this scam and penalized. A fine of $50 million and jail time for the chairman was recommended. Similarly, America's claim to infamy came through one of its most innovative companies, Enron. Shareholders lost around $70 billion and more than a thousand employees lost their retirement benefits and jobs.

A close scrutiny of these scams often shows how senior employees who danced with the devil become hostage to the situation and in turn held others hostage. Companies guilty of financial misappropriation and the employees who were willing to be part of these frauds would predominantly fall under one or more of the hostage syndromes explained in Chapter 2: Complexities/Dynamics of Globalization in Indian Context.

Habitually, these companies and their top executives come across as industry doyens but tend to wreck others to further their own selfish interests. This behaviour has been on the rise, leading to more avarice and creating an exaggerated sense of self-importance. Although marginalizing others may initially make them captors, they will gradually set themselves up to be taken hostage by their own devious schemes.

Lack of Willingness to Learn

Is learning time-consuming? Is it a formidable task, or is it painful, as a few opine? Learning is ubiquitous and pervasive. It can happen anywhere—at the workplace, in the airport, at the supermarket—just about anywhere. Learning, in a limited sense, can be described as a process of translating one's experience for a positive change in one's behaviour in the longer term. However, there are always people who reluctant to learn and remain in a constant state of turmoil.

In one of my sensitivity training programmes, I remember a participant and friend of mine asked me, 'When everything is fine, why should I waste my time learning? Learning is just painful.' I understood when he said 'learning' he meant 'changing'. Thanks to his attitude, it was disheartening to watch him go through numerous mishaps (and painfully overcome them) in his entrepreneurial journey.

The progress report of unsuccessful companies relates

to poor and autocratic leadership and their inappropriate policies. Learning from mistakes is the key to evolution and creativity, yet the evidence often goes unnoticed and ignored by others.

A 'learning organization' is the collective effort of individuals. It is no accident that most organizations learn poorly. The way they are designed and managed, the way people's jobs are defined, and most importantly, the way we have all been taught to think and interact create fundamental learning disabilities. Learning disabilities are tragic in children, especially when they go undetected. They are no less tragic in organizations, where they also go largely undetected.[28]

It is the responsibility of a leader to build a culture of learning across an organization, for rest assured, any letdown will destroy the company's future and its employees. Those who perpetuate shortcuts and quick fixes as strategies are likely to see only the mirage of success. For such people, excelling in their field or career is much like chasing an elusive dream.

When people enter the corporate world, unfortunately they neglect spending time understanding themselves. It has somehow become acceptable to state 'I have no time for myself'! The importance we give to our professional and social life over our personal life is worrisome, and can create an enormous imbalance. Perhaps, if we know ourselves better, we will change our perception of worldly success. The Buddha spoke of success as ephemeral and

---

[28]Senge, Peter M., 'Chapter 2: Does Your Organization Have a Learning Disability?' *op. cit.*, p. 17.

impermanent. It surely cannot be limited to money, material gain, status or power. It is about time to start looking inward before we go seeking answers outside.

6

The Myth of Impermanence

Buddhism views impermanence as a concept, which is 'an undeniable and inescapable fact of human existence from which nothing that belongs to this earth is ever free.' I cherish this wisdom and try to practise the Buddha's ever-luminescent dictum, 'Decay is inherent in all component things and existence is in a flux and a continuous becoming.'[29]

If only the importance of the above statements was deeply embedded in our minds and souls, we would probably suffer less, both physically and mentally. Sure, there are many who may be aware of this truth, but that's where it stops, with awareness. I have come across articles that talk about the anguish and despair even Buddhist monks found themselves in, after the Buddha's death. While life and existence are accepted to be in a flux, humans have conveniently ignored the 'becoming' part. The intellectual

[29]U Ba Khin, Thray Sithu Sayagyi, 'The Essentials of Buddha Dhamma in Meditative Practice', *Access to Insight*, 1995, https://tinyurl.com/49kj2sfh. Accessed on 6 May 2025.

concept of life being in a flux, hardly ever translates into pragmatism.

A study funded by Zurich University found that on an average, '45,000 suicides occur worldwide due to unemployment-related issues.' According to the study's lead, Dr Carlos Nordt of Zurich University's psychiatric hospital, 'It is not just losing the job but the stress and uncertainty, months before it happens, when companies might be looking to make redundancies that cause suicides.'[30] [31] We live in such impermanence as humans and will continue to be so. Nonetheless, how many of us can admit we consciously coexist with this impermanence without ever acknowledging it?

Comparing our life to a river would be the easiest analogy. A river's ongoing movement consists of a series of continual yet different moments. It travels from cause to cause, effect to effect, point to point and from one state of existence to another. The outward impression it creates is that of one continuous and unified passage, whereas in reality that is not so. The name of the river may stay the same, but it never is the same river if you tread on it each day. The river of this moment will never be the river of the next. The same goes for life—it is constantly changing, becoming something else from moment to moment.

---

[30]Nordt, Carlos, et al., 'Modelling Suicide and Unemployment: A Longitudinal Analysis Covering 63 Countries, 2000–11,' *The Lancet Psychiatry*, Vol. 2, No. 3, March 2015, pp. 239–245, https://tinyurl.com/yrvtvaxm. Accessed on 6 May 2025.

[31]Boseley, Sarah, 'Unemployment causes 45,000 suicides a year worldwide, finds study,' *The Guardian*, 11 February 2015, https://tinyurl.com/3scepx52. Accessed on 2 June 2025.

I have occasional bouts of intense nostalgia. Every time, I find the need to relive my childhood in the warmth of my native town. During one such spell, I yearned to go back fifty years, back to the roads I once roamed about freely, back to the shops in front of which I had once stood, back to the cafés where I once sat... I fulfilled this desire twice by visiting my native town. During each experience, standing on the same roads, in front of the same shops, sitting in the same café benches was absolutely dissatisfying. It was an utter and total disappointment and loss. The place was the same, yet it was not the same. There was a change in the environment, a change in the people and above all, a change in my feelings. It dawned on me then that impermanence is not only about loss, it is also about change. Hoping feelings shall always remain unchanged is far removed from actuality. A simple change in us changes our experiences and brings forth a profound learning that it wasn't the town you missed, but your childhood.

There are different perspectives on dealing with change. What is real is the existing moment, the present and that always is a result of the past. The human mind tends to conceive the past and present happenings as isolated incidents whereas in reality they are unified. Cause and effect are easy to understand yet we don't train ourselves to look at the cause in the effect.

The ordinary perception of our world is always fixed. We prefer to stay in familiar places with their familiar comfort and sense of security. While this may be calming in some way, it leads to attachment: attachment to places, to materials and resources, to position and power. Why do people buy a luxury car and then continue to crave for something more expensive? Is it the need for comfort? Or snob value? Or could it be much more than that?

When we choose to live by others' expectations and the public's predictable norms, our societal image becomes our emblem. Our wavering façades are seen through the eyes of others and the virile feeling of ownership wreaks havoc in our lives.

The feeling of 'I have what others don't' or 'I have what few people have' is momentary and to a certain extent pretentious. Have you noticed how our interest fades quickly the moment we acquire something we have wanted?

The same applies to one's work life. Success is neither a summit nor a pinnacle. It is merely a process. We must learn from the reflections of successful people—there is emptiness after achievement. Be it King Asoka or Steve Jobs, their poignant messages are not to be construed as mere philosophical direction but rather as a compass to navigate the troubled ocean called life!

Sanguinity of Impermanence

Impermanence doesn't encourage inactivity; it propels people to explore, experiment and excel. One common denominator in companies like Reliance, Forever 21, Xerox and Nirma is that their leaders came from relatively modest backgrounds, just like Patricia Narayan and Prem Ganapathy, whose stories are equally inspiring.

Patricia Narayan

Thirty years ago, Patricia Narayan began selling snacks

from a mobile cart on Chennai's Marina Beach, at a time when her personal life was in turmoil—a husband who was an addict, a failing marriage, and two young children to look after. Against all odds, she slowly built her way up, and today she runs a chain of restaurants employing over two hundred people. In an interview with *Rediff.com*, she recalled how she moved from cycle rickshaws to autos, and eventually to her own car, watching her daily earnings grow from a mere fifty paise to ₹2 lakh.[32] Receiving the FICCI Woman Entrepreneur of the Year award in 2010 came as a surprise, marking the first time her years of hard work had been formally recognized. It made her pause, reflect, and relive the long journey that brought her here. Now, her focus is on growing the Sandeepha brand she built from scratch.

Prem Ganapathy

Prem Ganapathy was left stranded at Bandra station in Mumbai by the very person with whom he had travelled. Prem was unfamiliar with the city, the language, and without any contacts. A fellow kind-hearted Tamilian took him to a temple and requested worshippers to help fund his return ticket to Chennai, but Prem chose to stay back and began working in a small restaurant, cleaning utensils. What began as a survival strategy gradually turned into a stepping stone—he moved from being a dishwasher to a tea

[32]Warrier, Shobha, 'From 50 Paise, She Now Earns Rs 200,000 a Day', *Rediff.com*, last updated on 8 June 2010, https://tinyurl.com/u38ywmus. Accessed on 30 May 2025.

boy, eventually becoming a partner, and then the founder of his own dosa restaurant. Over time, he built Dosa Plaza, known for its hundred and eight varieties of dosa and its network of franchises in India and abroad, making his journey a remarkable story of grit and determination.

Perhaps, what is evident in the above stories is the manner in which they learnt the all-important lesson of impermanence in life. The lesson of impermanence in life offers not only challenges but hope too.

Challenges of Impermanence

When the tech giant Cognizant announced job cuts in October 2019, IT employees across India and the world felt the aftershocks. Both Cognizant and other IT firms' employees fell into a similar pattern of sleepless nights triggered by anxiety. A few even engaged in legal proceedings through collective effort. The importance of this issue was palpable. Various media outlets encouraged discussions and networks arranged for talk shows.

I had the opportunity to chair one such talk show on a prominent regional TV network. The discussion focused primarily on the announcement of lay-off of employees and the number of employees who would be axed (claimed by participants to be around seven to eight thousand) and the consequent nervousness about the outcome. It was shocking to me that only during such a time were people actually opening up to the possibility of the impermanence of their job.

Participants who were recently laid off steered the conversation into difficult waters. The pathos shared by those in senior positions was heart-rending. While the reason for the lay-offs was logical by industry standards, it was illogical for the employees. The only silver lining in all this gloom was the fact that employees were slowly catching up with reality—the reality of impermanence. The challenge in such a situation is facing this impermanence and gaining some maturity while handling the consequent distress.

While the challenges are different for employers and employees, the concern remains the same—survival. The challenges for employers and employees are both dynamic, integrated and mutually inclusive. Can there be a more powerful lesson on impermanence than what Covid has taught us?

Lack of Clarity

An inherent quality of impermanence is lack of clarity. People who insist on clarity before they set out on a task are usually those who become comfortable with the daily humdrum, take fewer risks, and often find the need to depend on people around them. Lack of clarity does not necessarily impede one's cognitive skill. Instead, it facilitates ingenuity and augments innovativeness. It powers us to reach beyond limits.

When Neil Armstrong and Buzz Aldrin set foot on the moon, Richard Nixon, the then President of the United States, had his speechwriter prepare condolences in the event they were marooned in the vast space. After Armstrong's historic announcement, 'one small step for man, one giant leap for mankind,' both astronauts returned to the lunar module, upon completion of their historic task. With the American flag now permanently planted on the moon's surface, both men were eager to return, when they noticed a switch on a crucial circuit breaker had been damaged. This was the only way they could manually start the engine, so they decided to get some rest while the mission control team at NASA tried to repair it from Earth.

Unfortunately, luck would not be on their side. Aldrin was running out of patience when he decided to take matters into his own hands and jammed a pen into the circuit breaker to make a makeshift switch. To everyone's surprise, this spontaneous solution was probably what saved the day. Both men launched off from the surface of the moon safely. This story only goes to show that adaptable thinkers and constant innovators are often born during times of crises and change. Nothing really lasts forever.

A person who embraces impermanence in a culture of change and looks at it as an opportunity often emerges as a leader. Unexpected events—a sudden change, a new boss, being pushed to take on new roles, maybe even a merger between companies—produce uncertainty and obscurity. Lack of clarity is a prominent feature of a VUCA-filled (volatility, uncertainty, complexity, ambiguity) environment. Any approach we make to face VUCA challenges means dealing with lack of clarity.

Fluidity

Lack of clarity leaves us with no option except to be pushed into a state of fluidity. For people who prefer to work with an agenda or plan, fluidity is never an advantage. There is a world of difference working with the required/desired resources and working with available resources. Simply enabling the required resources with good planning does not pose any significant challenge. Training and practice make task handling easy, but things hardly go as planned.

While necessity is the mother of invention, divergent thinking requires a certain mental make-up for all. To quote an apt example, Covid has familiarized is with many hybrid methods of conducting our classroom sessions, conferences, and training programmes. Our experience with this kind of fluidity will certainly help us forge an apt mental constitution. Fluidity simply enhances one's capacity to anticipate and one's preparedness for facing risks and expect the unexpected (*as is* instead of *as if*).

Organizations that are rigid in their policies, culture and processes are constantly challenged by the ever-changing dynamics of the global market. On a larger scale, government sanctions tend to alter the geo-political climate, which, like a domino effect, affects organizations and their employees. Neither organizations nor individuals can afford to see fluidity as a negative phenomenon. That would only serve to impede any positive change or opportunities.

The dual need to maintain stability in the face of shocks and to leverage the existing optimization is very significant, while responding to changing markets, and resolving increasing challenges. The end result is the deliverance of more innovation that tackles these changes successfully. This requires both fluidity in thinking and stability in approach.

This inevitable fluid situation affects almost everyone,

ranging from fresh recruits to key company cogs. While offer letters are being sent to new recruits, existing employees are 'on the bench' with salary, but no experience to back that up, particularly in IT companies. Alternative thinking acts as a significant leeway for those stuck in their unshakeable belief in stability. Regrettably, people seldom seek alternatives due to their belief that things will remain the same forever.

As opposed to fluidity, rigidity holds on to tried and tested thoughts, habits and behaviour, all ill-placed in a dynamic environment. A believer of rigidity may attain immediate comfort sans alternative strategies to swim against the tide. Such people will soon find themselves stuck in functional fixedness.

Multiskilling

The effects of impermanence pretty much permeate every aspect of the day. Projects being withheld, postponements without an end date...the list is never-ending. The bottom line is, existing manpower is rationed and reduced. The compulsion to maximize productivity with minimum resources becomes normal and acceptable. The ones left fretting in such scenarios are the ones who are highly specialized or 'mono-skilled'. The management tends to identify and give preference to those who normally have multiple skills, which makes business sense, but the important question to ask is whether the mono-skilled will get sensitized to this need and if yes, how soon?

Today multitasking or being multiskilled is almost a strategy used to prevent retrenchment. It is no longer just confined to the lower rung of the corporate ladder and is fast getting integrated at all levels of management.

Expertise in supply-chain management will be far more preferable than expertise in logistics. A win-win situation, if you will. The management is assured of quality deliverables and the employees improve their 'marketability'. Multiskilled personnel become synonymous with optimal manpower rationalization while also offering other benefits to themselves.

- Flexibility and minimization of disruption
- Non-redundancy
- Less anxiety about job insecurity
- Increased market value

It is no surprise that employees with multitasking abilities have better chances of survival than others, even in dire situations. While industries undergo multiple disruptions, existing jobs may disappear and specialists may become a special breed. Mindful of cost rationalization, companies would much rather hire generalists who are quick to adapt and become jacks of all trades.

All this said, the issue to deal with comes in the form of 'forced' multitasking. There will be no learning if being multiskilled is not achieved by one's own volition. Organizations should engage in and practise multiskilled learning at the levels of both the management and the employees. Exploiting any multiskilled employee with the sole aim of saving cost is fraught with inevitable pitfalls and to be honest, unfair. Forced multiskill training will rob people of their key strengths and engage them in less competent areas resulting in resistance. An electrician can be trained to become a mechanic so long as the employee consents; only then can it be considered an effective strategy.

Role Evaporation

An employee's role does not exist in vacuum. It is dependent primarily on organizational expectations and stakeholders' demands. Any company operating in these fluid times, with little to no preparedness will end up going haywire. In other words, this would be one of the biggest challenges arising from a state of impermanence.

Digital technology and employment are more interconnected now than ever before. The challenges for companies in this advanced digital landscape are ever-present. It would definitely be unfathomable to forecast how digital experiences may alter our basic way of life—both personal and official. Artificial intelligence and machine learning are already replacing existing and outdated technologies, leaving hardly much to say about their impact on the job market, specifically in redefining the role of people in an organization.

Even as theories have circulated on the internet for a long time about Motorola's failure, an interesting thing to note was how their obstinacy may have played a role in the failure. Their innovativeness tapered off, and their failure to understand their consumer preferences was too big to ignore. It has been a while since we have changed from buying technology purely as a hardware decision to something of a software decision now. We want to run apps, play games and be connected socially—all at the same time. Our attention has long shifted from hardware to software solutions, and market differentiation instead.

Evaporation as we all know is akin to metamorphosis, even transformation. Water changing to gas or vapour from its liquid form is not simply an act of disappearance, it can be considered a change in form too.

In reality, organizations are nothing but people, and if managers are not transformed, the business will simply vanish. An ever-changing digital world needs creative thinking and application. No manager can sit in an unchanging role for years to come. And those who tend to, are bound to have poor sensitization and blame others for their immobility. While they cry over the erosion of their role, unbeknownst to them, role evaporation has already started to take place.

Unless managers develop creative thinking and be open to learning, there will be no transformation. Within this context, role evaporation has the ability to transform a person and bring about new role definitions, energies and strategies, thereby ensuring that such a person becomes better suited to the changing environment.

Mobility

A detour or en route, a career trajectory can be categorized by either. A detour makes mobility 'enforced'. This can be either self-imposed or thrust on an employee by their employer. On the other hand, en route can make excellent 'evolutionary' en routers, who are usually learners and seekers, and who are energized by the joy of the journey instead.

Detour

A detour can be defined as a roundabout, a circuitous way. It can also mean a side road, byway, evasion or excuse. In our context, it can be inferred that an individual's growth trajectory is not always organic/natural; career paths are often enforced with artificial growth and empty patches.

For example, shifting an employee from one location to another, one counter to another or one project to another without their consent symbolizes forced mobility. I do not wish to give the impression of being against locational transfers or mobility. I am aware that technology has redefined most of our contemporary businesses, with its effects permeating globally. Wage disparity, shortage of skills, non-viability of a business in a particular location and the need for effective leadership all demand people to move. The move would be worthwhile if the mobility is consensual. It could be a replacement, a versatility transfer or a remedial transfer.

I understand that organizational mobility is a debatable subject but I would like to add that experiences often show forced mobility does not yield productivity. When an employee transfer is made by management as a punishing tool, it is a double whammy. Neither side benefits. Case studies abound that correlate forced transfers and the subsequent sabotage engineered by employees.

En route

En route, as an evolutionary mobility, is crafted and created by the manager for one's career advancement and passion.

When a vision is crafted, it encompasses a path for a long-term career journey. A journey is not commenced if one is not mobile. Mobility is not limited to physical movement alone; it can signify our psychological movement, a boundaryless mindset which is a prerequisite for one's growth.

A boundaryless career mindset is characterized by varying levels of physical and psychological movements. Sullivan, Defillippi and Arthur developed the boundaryless career concept as a response to changes in the direction of more permeable (organizational) boundaries.[33] The boundaryless career attitude refers to organizational mobility preference (i.e. people's physical mobility) and a boundaryless mindset (i.e. people's psychological mobility).[34]

Organizational mobility preference is reflected in one's readiness to conduct actual moves between different occupations, jobs, and organizations. People with a high organizational mobility preference choose to work in several different organizations and actually cross organizational boundaries by taking up employment in different companies. In contrast, a boundaryless mindset refers to an individual's mental ability to be mobile. A person with a boundaryless

---

[33]Sullivan, S.E., and M.B. Arthur, 'The evolution of the boundaryless career concept: Examining physical and psychological mobility', *Journal of Vocational Behavior*, 69(1), 2009, p. 9, https://tinyurl.com/yt8p7uur. Accessed on 30 May 2025.

[34]Defillippi, Robert J., and Michael B. Arthur, 'The boundaryless career: A competency-based perspective', *Journal of Organizational Behavior*, Vol. 15, No. 4, 1994, pp. 307–324, *Wiley*, https://tinyurl.com/4de46yu2. Accessed on 30 May 2025.

mindset enjoys working on projects with people across many organizations and feels energized and enthusiastic about engaging in new experiences and situations outside the organizations too.

Protean Career Attitude

In bringing more perspective to this concept, I see the relevance of the protean career concept that was introduced by Douglas T. Hall as a reaction to changing career pathways that contained more freedom and growth as well as self-determination for individuals.[35] Although sometimes protean career and boundaryless career have been used interchangeably, the constructs have different meanings.[36] A boundaryless career attitude is characterized by high psychological and/or physical mobility. A protean career attitude implies that a person strives towards a developmental progression and self-fulfilment.

Protean is a synonym for being flexible, adaptive, and changeable. The protean career is defined 'as a career in which the person is 1) value-driven in the sense that the person's internal values provide the guidance and measure of success for the individual's career; and 2) self-directed in personal career management, having the ability to be

---

[35]Hall, Douglas T, 'The protean career: A quarter-century journey', *Journal of Vocational Behavior*, Vol. 65, No. 1, 2004, pp. 1–13, https://tinyurl.com/39uuthrb. Accessed on 2 June2025.

[36]Hall, Douglas T., 'Protean Career', *CareerMarcr*, 1976, https://tinyurl.com/mrkms454. Accessed on 2 June 2025.

adaptive in terms of performance and learning demands.[37] People with a protean career attitude are value-driven as they shape their careers according to their own internal values and beliefs in contrast to, for example, organizational values and beliefs, and they are self-directed as they pursue their careers based on personally defined career goals. People with a protean career attitude rely on their personal values and aspirations as a guide for career decisions.

Protean and boundaryless career attitudes can be considered as key drivers that can indirectly affect career outcomes through actual behaviour. For example, placing a high value on a protean career attitude might result in higher goal-setting and a greater investment of effort because one feels responsible for one's career and wants to act according to one's own values and aspirations. Also, a boundaryless and protean career mindset enables a manager to look at their career beyond a single career setting, internally or externally. This mindset enhances a manager's scope for learning multiple skills, and this adaptability, in turn, makes for a wholesome leader, ready to lead any organization.

It is interesting to note how a lack of this mindset drives even high potential managers to resist relocations and to voluntarily become victims of psychological immobility and inertia.

Sensing this backdrop, Hall suggests that it is imperative to focus primarily on the subjective perspective

---

[37]Briscoe, Jon P., and Douglas T. Hall, 'The Interplay of Boundaryless and Protean Careers: Combinations and Implications', *Journal of Vocational Behavior*, Vol. 69, No. 1, 2006, pp. 4–18, https://tinyurl.com/4d6hhhda. Accessed on 3 June 2025.

of an individual's career based on one's defined goals encompassing the whole life space, as well as on being driven by psychological success rather than objective success such as pay, rank, or power.[38]

[38]'Protean Career', *IResearchNet*, https://tinyurl.com/3wmpet28. Accessed on 2 June 2025.

7

Calamitous Disruption

If disaster becomes the cause, change is no longer an alternative but the only response. There is no option other than to change or perish! Disruption could be voluntary or it could be thrust upon us. There have been several instances where progressive organizations have engineered disruptions voluntarily in their products, processes and services for their sustenance. This has enabled them to outshine their competitors, enrich their customers' experiences, and improve their organizational well-being.

Outwardly, such disruptions are not seen as positive by many, yet they present opportunities for the imaginative few. Organizations across industries face disruption. The key is to turn disruption into an opportunity rather than letting it become a threat.[39] Progressive organizations and their employees prefer to welcome disruption rather than be afraid of it.

---

[39]Woodson, John, 'Disruption: Opportunity or Threat?', *Harvard Business School Online*, 23 July 2015, https://tinyurl.com/2s3w9mc3. Accessed on 6 May 2025.

But the characteristics of forced disruptions like Covid are different. Though it was a calamity, yet the human mind considered this as an unwelcome disruption (disaster) and tried to overcome it. Covid will not be easily erased from our collective memory, as the post-Covid era taught us many lessons in our personal, organizational and social lives.

Covid threw up a hostage situation on multiple fronts, compelling organizations and employees to handle its impact in every sphere of life.

Disruptions and Lessons Learned

Remote Working: Unequivocal Priority of People's Well-Being

Across the globe, boardrooms, office corridors and town hall meetings that would usually reverberate with demands, rather commandments such as 'I don't care what you do; I need an increase in productivity and improved financials', fell silent during Covid—no one was around to listen. Many business meetings turned into SOS meetings, all on virtual mode.

People never felt this close to their near and dear ones. Irrespective of rank and file, every employee wanted to move closer to their families. At times, people weren't allowed to visit their own parents and kith and kin out of the desperate desire to protect each other. For many, including myself, it was a touch-and-go situation. The fear of death was writ large on everyone's face. Hapless migrant workers abandoned their jobs to trek miles cross-country in the absence of any transport, only to be able to return to their families in the villages. Many never made it. Employers were no exception to this desperate state of affairs.

The Covid pandemic didn't just rattle health systems—it shook the foundations of how businesses operated across the globe. Many employers found themselves completely unprepared for a crisis of this scale, struggling to respond as the familiar rhythms of work completely came undone overnight. Remote work, once a perk or a back-up plan, was the only option—yet most organizations lacked the skill or the mindset to manage the new set-up effectively, especially when it came to keeping up the collective morale. As lockdowns were imposed hastily as emergency measures, countless businesses around the world were forced to shut shop, leading to sweeping lay-offs—at times with severance, but mostly without. What emerged wasn't just an operational scramble but a reckoning: companies had to rethink everything, from how they ran their day-to-day business to how they treated their employees. By many accounts, the economic blow dealt by Covid-19 was far harder than the 2008 financial crisis, leaving organizations with no choice but to redraw their playbooks.[40]

People across generations had to live through this nightmare that forced many (employers and employees) to prioritize their lives as well as the well-being of their near and dear ones, over money, material possessions and

---

[40]de Waal, Andre, Jeroen Linthorst, and Charlotte Hetterschijt, 'Lessons Learned by Organisations during the Covid-19 Pandemic', *International Journal of Management and Applied Research*, Vol. 8, No. 1, 2021, pp. 72–90, https://tinyurl.com/3mbjjrpd. Accessed on 6 May 2025.

mindless consumerism. 'People first and foremost' was all that mattered.

Style of Working: Emergence of WFH

It is an understatement to say that Covid-19 had a huge impact on the job market. The belief that on-site working alone could improve productivity was challenged and partially nullified. The advent of WFH and the shift to tele-work has changed our working style. Several surveys during and after Covid have suggested that many companies were able to maintain their optimum level of productivity, while some companies registered an uptick in their performance and productivity. The level of productivity, of course, varied and was industry-specific. However, service sectors like tourism, insurance, retail, hospitality, aviation, manufacturing, automobiles, etc., took a body-blow. At the same time, hospitals and pharma companies did brisk business, the unfortunate trade-off for such industries being the unprecedented scale of people's ill health and desperate fight for survival.

Though initially WFH faced several setbacks—technical and otherwise—many employees saw it as a blessing in disguise as they were able to become *part of the family* again. While some organizations witnessed a loss in productivity, they saved on infrastructural and indirect employee costs. Many IT employees hailing from rural and urban areas were able to save on rent, conveyance and other logistics as they stayed put in their native places. The remote-work option seemed to suit them. The preference for WHF still continues.

Post Covid, IT companies like Tata Consultancy Services (TCS) have urged all employees to come to the office to work. Employees' resistance to go to the office is still an issue for many companies. As per TCS's official statement, around seventy per cent of the workforce has returned to office. However, employees of smaller IT and ITES (information technology-enabled service) companies, especially those who live outside cities, insisted on working from home as they found leaving the comfort of home, incurring expenditure of rent, conveyance, and missing their family challenging. All in all, the post-Covid era has witnessed the emergence of two distinct beliefs and practices:

1. It is worth trying a hybrid model (part-WFH, part-WFO—work from office).
2. An organization's productivity need not fall if a robust remote-monitoring system is in place.

The advantages of the hybrid working model could override certain disadvantages like disengagement of personal touch and minimized collaborative space of the employees, as many favour the hybrid working model.

The advantages of WFH are:

- Better work-life balance
- Flexibility in working hours
- Saved travel time used to optimize productivity
- Less stressed-out family life due to the working family member's presence at home

The disadvantages are:

- Absence of interaction with the team and co-workers possible only in person in office

- Work done largely in isolation
- A thin line between work and family time
- Increased stress while handling people and schedules (at home and in office)

Executives who were earlier not used to the performance of their team being 'remote monitored' became sceptical and indulged in toxic behaviour in their professional relationships. The remote-working situation has led several organizations to take certain measures.

With a shift in organizational design, it was imperative to move from the conventional management of teams to their remote management. Remote working and remote management of employees' performance come with their own challenges and dynamics, and need time for evolutionary growth. Challenges and practices are redefining the ways of working, and of managing teams today. Tools like Google Meet, Zoom, etc., are go-to platforms for team coordination and participation. However, managers, executives and rest of the workforce had, and continue to have their share of doubts and stress, even with this model.

Many managers felt inadequate managing the performance of their teams effectively as the members were remotely stationed. Their major doubt was that people were not managing their time effectively, resulting in poor performance and reduced productivity. This suspicion drove many managers to indulge in unbecoming behaviour, while constantly nudging their subordinates, adding to the stress on both sides.

Many managers live by the belief that constant direction and supervision of executives can yield higher outputs. Such managers do not believe in delegating work or in enabling their teams to handle greater responsibilities independently. Therefore, there is a constant volley of communication between the team members and its leaders. Quick learners in the team understand that a higher level of *work delegation* to subordinates is imperative for a speedy and effective decision-making process.

It was tough for managers to learn how to equip themselves to handle their teams effectively under the new circumstances. Life in the virtual space is a reality and appropriate training programmes teach the workforce the ways to use it effectively. Non-IT companies, which were not exposed to offshore managing teams, had to learn new strategies to bring change in themselves and in their teams. Besides the changes in organizational and managerial behaviour, prolonged periods of isolation also resulted in a reduced sense of belonging to the organization.

Experience proves that diversity and chaos are healthy for team-building and bonding. Reflective experiences of ups and downs make people realize their strengths and weaknesses. I have personally heard managers talk about 'how the change in their beliefs enhanced trust among their team members which hitherto was missing.' They did share that post-Covid they had offloaded their micro-management style, thereby promoting greater trust and accountability among their team members.

Shift in Bargaining Power: Redefinition of the Purpose of Working and Change in Strategies

In many countries, a certain level of the workforce and job-seekers still has the bargaining power. During the Covid-19 pandemic, many workers, especially those with low income or modest education, were less likely to negotiate their salaries with their employers. This was largely due to increased job insecurity and the possibility of reduced earnings. On the contrary, workers with high levels of education appeared more confident about bargaining, most likely because the demand for high-skilled labour remained strong.

There is a deep generational divide in the willingness to bargain with employers. Older workers were less inclined to ask for a pay hike in light of the pandemic. Nearly one-third of the essential workers received a pay hike because of the risks they had taken during the pandemic to keep businesses running. The more comfortable essential workers are asking for a raise, the more likely they are to receive it. Workers' willingness to bargain with their employers is a critical indicator of their collective bargaining power. Understanding the strength of workers' bargaining power sheds light on employment trends and income outcomes as the economy gradually recovers from the Covid pandemic.

Among other disruptions, the pandemic is expected to have lasting consequences for the Indian labour market. An increase in the 'unemployed workers pool' will possibly reduce their bargaining power and wages. The introduction of new labour codes in India seeks to, on the face of it, consolidate multiple labour laws and simplify the process of providing social security, safety and occupational health. However, this has also raised concerns about workers' bargaining power. The Industrial Relations Code, 2020, introduces stricter regulations on workers' right to strike work, grants employers greater flexibility in hiring and firing, overlooks the needs of unorganized workers, and opens the door to possible extension of working hours, among other concerns. However, the Code was passed without a tripartite consultation and meaningful engagement.[41] While certain clauses are beneficial to workers, the law has almost done away with workers' rights on their bargaining power.

The Indian and global employment market continues to deal with fluctuations and unpredictability. White-collar hiring remains stable in India, with an uptick in hiring for artificial intelligence (AI) and machine learning (ML) roles.[42] Large-scale lay-offs have taken place recently in prominent Indian companies such as Ola Electric[43] and JioHotstar.[44] In the US, employees are being laid off across hundred and sixty companies in sectors ranging from retail and pharma to airlines, and including Walmart, Morgan Stanley, and Pfizer, to name a few.[45]

---

[41]Narayan, Priti, and R. Geetha, 'New labour codes rewrite workers' rights, but here's where they go wrong', *The Times of India*, 17 March 2025, https://tinyurl.com/bdzf3fkw. Accessed on 5 June 2025.

[42]Naukri Content Team, 'Understanding Hiring Trends with Naukri JobSpeak Report – May 2025', *naukri.com*, 12 June 2025, https://tinyurl.com/47yxhe2x. Accessed on 1 August 2025.

[43]Tejaswi, Mini, 'Ola Electric's lay-offs rattle India's growing EV job market', *The Hindu*, 26 March 2025, https://tinyurl.com/mryhcbmc. Accessed on 5 June 2025.

[44]HT News Desk, 'JioStar to lay off over 1,100 with overlapping roles after merger: Report', *Hindustan Times*, 7 March 2025, https://tinyurl.com/2nts2rxh. Accessed on 5 June 2025.

[45]ET Online, 'Morgan Stanley, Walmart, Pfizer and More: Full List of over 150 American Companies Laying Off Employees in June', *The Economic Times*, 2 June 2025, https://tinyurl.com/bdp3543p. Accessed on 5 June 2025.

In recent years, I have learnt from my corporate clients about an increasingly alarming trend—attrition across manufacturing, automobiles, and the service sector. The trend is more marked among the Gen Z. Gone are the days when engineers were preferred for first-line/supervisory roles. Today, managements prefer diploma holders instead of engineers as the latter seem overqualified or are considered unstable. If this situation continues, engineers are likely to encounter speed breakers while seeking their preferred employment.

While bargaining power is a contentious matter between employers and employees, boardrooms are busy changing their strategies to minimize cost and to lessen the bargaining power of the workforce. One game-changing strategy now used in manufacturing, including in original equipment manufacturer (OEM) companies, is replacing permanent manpower with trainees and contract workers.

Employees have realized what they really need from organizations is employee well-being over monetary benefits for their work. Wisdom has dawned on them; money is not the only criteria they are after! Thus the true purpose of employment has been redefined.

Part IV

Liberation

Slavery is the next thing to hell

—HARRIET TUBMAN

8

Liberating the Mind

If history has taught us anything, it is that the forerunner of any freedom movement is a liberated mind. Leaders who nurtured the vision of independence began by first seeding the virtue of liberation among people. This step—liberation of the mind—has created more warriors and patriots who have sacrificed their personal and communal life for a far larger cause. Yet, when the songs of liberation reverberate in the air, their losses become healing memories. Being aware of the lasting consequences at multiple levels of their life has never deterred them from fighting for their cause. The joy of being liberated is soul-stirring; it is a joy that humanity has experienced on multiple occasions.

Is it erroneous to conclude that when people fight for their nation's independence, their personal liberty is compromised? Is the willingness to forgo one's personal right to liberty, power to believe, act and express, the worst misery to invite upon oneself? Social psychologists would point out several reasons that prevent an individual from fighting for their personal freedom. Paradoxically, the grit and valour demonstrated during the fight for a country's freedom is often missing while seeking personal freedom.

The collective conscience of a nation often fails to deliver when it comes to using it for an individual's liberation; in the long run this tends to disrupt democratic processes. Both the physical and psychological liberation of an individual are significant as choosing liberty is the most non-coercive choice anyone needs to exercise for a healthy and wholesome life.

Kill the Enemy Within

Personal liberty can never be achieved without liberation of the mind. This is probably more evident in those who pursue their achievement-oriented careers while leading a life that flounders philosophically.

The comfort achieved through career advancement often vies for status quo. When this is questioned, it often means one has to accommodate discomfort and anxiety. The thin veil of comfort around an individual is often seen as a protective cover rather than what it really is—a vicious trap. While much has been written about people who have sacrificed their lives for their country, few can deny that they resist liberating themselves. How many of us can speak of having read or heard about people who have fought the enemy within? Misplaced beliefs and personal values have led many to become non-reflective.

Many talented people live according to other people's ideas about life, often at the cost of their personal desires and strengths. This often results in a lack of faith in their own capabilities. Career fanatics are not the only ones in this club.

At home or elsewhere, often people are brought up to believe 'acting out' is more normative than 'acting on/in'. Both psychological terms, *acting out* is the process of impulsively expressing our unconscious thoughts, usually in a way that harms others. The reaction could be spontaneous as a defence mechanism, to avoid reflecting on one's own anxiety and discomfort associated with one's unconscious feelings. Two familial examples illustrate this clearly: 1) If parents are afraid of their adolescent child habitually coming home late at night, they vent their anger instead of their fear. 2) Many children choose their careers due to external and/or parental influence, suppressing their own interests.

Acting on/in arises out of our inner feelings; any outward action is only a means to express our inner feeling without distortion. There is conformity between *in* and *out* as we express from our inner space, consciously and effectively. If the parents had expressed their fear, saying, 'We are afraid of things happening out there and we will be happy if you come home early,' it could probably change the behaviour of the adolescent child as they too may empathize with their parents' feelings. The misplaced feeling of anger could do more harm to the child than good.

This early institutionalization shapes our mind as a non-believer in the self. Children grow up as they are expected to rather than as they truly are within, being constantly conscious of their limitations rather than their strength. Many risk-averse employees tend to act out rather than act in. The tendency to believe in one's own limitations have curtailed creativity and self-exploration. Potential and greatness are ignored and often go unrecognized.

Therefore, poor self-belief becomes an enemy within. It strengthens our resistance to liberating ourselves from the hostage situation—be it from 'directed' ourselves or from others. Liberation becomes an elusive dream. So, destroy the enemy within!

Often our enemy resides in our subconscious mind in the form of vague concepts and wrong perceptions about self and others, which we resist bringing up to our conscious mind. Only a few realize that it is our subconscious mind which drives us more than our conscious mind.

Subversion of the Subconscious

The subconscious mind is a power bank with unlimited power. The conscious mind is always subservient to the subconscious mind. Charging the conscious mind using power from the subconscious power bank needs to be done in the right way, failing which the former may run amok. If you are a budding speaker ready to address a crowd, you constantly need to assure yourself that you are confident and fearless. However, in the presence of an audience, you may have butterflies in your stomach and tend to become nervous or incoherent. This uncooperative behaviour of your subconscious mind can be altered through the proper alignment of intention between confidence and action. Should there be a conflict between the two, the outcome will tend to be undesirable. It is the same reason why people who indulge in bad habits struggle to let go of them.

Understanding our subconscious mind and its power is a privilege a select few enjoy; these people are habituated to looking within and reflecting. Until this happens, the subconscious mind remains underutilized in most cases. Discussions rarely revolve around this subject, and perhaps are even strategically circumvented by people with vested interests. Powerful people often deploy their power in ways that 'fallible' subordinates listen to, put up with, believe in, and to a great extent, obey or be subservient to. A tamed elephant does not realize its strength. Similarly, these subordinates are encouraged to remain unaware of their own strength and over time accept their condition as their final reality.

Such subservient subconscious minds are overrun with unverified beliefs. In that sense, humans are no different from animals. The few who control a community know all too well that if ordinary people's power is unleashed, the former's role will be challenged. Communal leaders and politicians never encourage getting in touch with your seat of power, also known as the subconscious mind. That is a well-oiled strategy to keep you down. Corporates are no different!

Think of a challenging situation that called for immediate action, and that you were able to handle effectively. Even though you felt elated to be the solution provider, each time, to who have you attributed this success? Is it to your self or to the superiors or to the omnipresent powers? Who here is the rightful claimant of that appreciation?

Faced with this question, you may notice your lifelong conditioning come into play. The conditioning, the belief that 'I am not responsible for my success' has always been an obstacle in realizing and recognizing our true strengths. Even animals sheltered in zoos vaguely understand they belong elsewhere but put up with the captivity for their survival. Are we any different from them?

While our subconscious mind plays a pivotal role in driving our actions and transactions, we have learnt to ignore it. How often have we seen that exemplary skills in many go unnoticed or suppressed for a lifetime? It becomes doubly harder to witness someone else snatch our credit. Our frustration remains unarticulated and tends to fester in the depths of our subconscious minds, without being able to surface.

The eternal quest to please our conscious mind never ceases. We are so entrenched in it, that we forget in the course of our lives to ever peek into our subconscious mind. We would be surprised by the amount the subconscious has to offer humankind, much like a well with abundant water waiting to satiate people's thirst. As the unconscious mind lies beneath the subconscious mind; bringing everything to conscious mind (awareness level) is a discomfiting process, one of finally knowing, discovering who we are and what we want to be!

What Is Your Bottom Line?

Has the thought of freeing yourself from your job (corporate and others) ever occurred to you? Better still, have you ever thought you should quit your job and do something which you are genuinely passionate about? If yes, then you are the one who needs to be liberated. Liberating oneself from a flustered work environment is more of a psychological phenomenon than a physical one. Though outwardly it doesn't raise much cause for concern, it undoubtedly casts a pall of gloom on our well-being if not attended to quickly enough.

The word 'liberation' is considered by many managers as something monumental, and they may be baffled when faced with it. This is also the point at which managers question the need for deliberation on liberation. With an agreed-upon agenda, one works in a company knowing full well that any benefit resulting thereof is a quid pro quo. If the consideration is mutual in terms of benefit, then why do managers (you) undergo stress and anxiety? Is the quantum of quid pro quo unequal? If yes, then who gains more and who gains less? If the company's bottom line is profit alone, then what is the bottom line for a manager?

The notion that only money matters, remains a mere motivation for immediate gratification rather than an enduring solution. The voices of those chasing money are stronger than of those who want well-being. This lack of focus on well-being compels us to create a culture of indifference where enablers of well-being are consistently compromised, even abused and derided.

Ironically, in the field of human development, people relate to their work with hardly any reflection or emotion, allowing themselves to be part of an accepted, 'unreflected' behaviour in the work space. The lesson here is that not only does our shadow (alter ego) contain those aspects of ourselves which we have chosen not to become; it also contains those aspects which we have not yet chosen to become.

Oppressor and Oppressed

Managers sublimate their thoughts into an organized behavioural pattern when it comes to dealing with others. This translates into oppression. When managers with these oppressive patterns surrender to regressive corporate etiquettes, it is both painful to watch and live through. When oppressed subordinates turn out to become oppressive superiors, an organizational culture with acceptable victimhood is perpetuated. The true account below may further our understanding of this psychological conditioning.

A friend asked renowned psychologist Marvin Zuckerman[46] why the Nazis were so successful in exterminating six million European Jews. Dismayed by his friend's attitude while he asked this question, nonetheless Zuckerman gave him a simple answer: A heavily armed superior force can do what it will with an unarmed civilian population surrounded by people who, at one end of the spectrum, are indifferent to their fate, and at the other end are hostile, happy to be rid of them, and are even willing to participate in their murder—with many in between who may be somewhat sympathetic but are afraid for their own lives. This is comparable with what happens in organizations. The oppressed and the oppressor surrender to their inability to resist or to submit to their self-created fate.

While it is incredibly painful to understand how hundreds of Jews passively accepted their destiny,

---

[46]Marvin Zuckerman is a retired professor of English and Yiddish at Los Angeles Valley College, and has written seven books, including two college textbooks. He is the founder of a literary agency and is active in the Southern California Workmen's Circle.
Zuckerman, Marvin, 'Why Were the Nazis So Successful at Killing Six Million Jews?' *Jewish Currents*, 18 April 2013, https://tinyurl.com/mr2eavj7. Accessed on 30 May 2025.

Zuckerman wonders whether the Jews were to be blamed for their presumed passivity and cooperation in their own murders. While the concept of 'blaming the victim' has no place in the Holocaust, the same cannot be said of an organizational set-up. The perpetuation of oppression is made possible by the conditioning of Gen X by the colonial mindset and of Gen Y by technology, by simply being both the oppressed and the oppressor.

While oppression is not articulated clearly in real terms, everyone is socialized into the oppressor-oppressed roles. These issues are not exactly boardroom concerns, as the buck is always passed on to senior executives for their management. When an attitude like this is socially accepted and empowered, it even functions as the justification for the continued mistreatment of all.

Oppression can either be forced or wilful (the will we refer to is executed by the oppressed). This wilful oppression implies that a significant number of employees suffer from a victim mentality and cannot (do not) see oppression as a precursor to slavery. They are subdued by the abusive behaviour of their superiors and remain in an uncomplaining mode. While some are aware of their state of being, many others remain unaware.

Wilful oppression in an unaware state is mild, subtle and full of grey areas. Much like several governments who offer freebies to the general public in the hope of securing vote banks. Another more contemporary example would be that of corporate oppression. Do we not belong to the era where privacy has been mortgaged? Our personal financial transactions, messages, private online behaviour and more have all been usurped by corporations. How many of us really read the 'Terms &Conditions' before hitting 'Accept'? Are we able to decode why TV ads disclose terms and conditions such as 'subject to market risks' so swiftly?! What is the guarantee that we will not be exploited by these companies to improve their business interests? While these are real threats, we wilfully choose not to heed them while the damage continues to be inflicted unchecked. This form of social oppression being an important topic, we shall now focus on the corporate set-up.

The existence of known and unknown forms of victimhood in organizations is not uncommon. Any retribution from top management for senior executives' failures is passed down verbatim by these executives to their juniors. This is either accompanied by the same or increased level of emotional threats. The failure could be due to a variety of reasons, but the cross is borne by junior employees. This is where the statement 'The oppressors oppress the oppressed' rings true.

A good performer is expected to work more; in other words, a good performer is 'punished' for their performance. The good performer is either cajoled into working more or simply enjoys the recognition. Both are poor examples of good governance. Unless one wants to liberate themselves from victimhood, the exploitation continues. The liberation we refer to here is the outcome of certain affirmative action and concerted behaviour of both senior and junior employees. For the feudal outlook to change, our assumptions and beliefs about our own selves needs to be corrected first.

Servant Leadership

The term 'servant leadership' was coined by Robert K. Greenleaf, a twentieth-century researcher who was sceptical about traditional leadership styles that focused on more authoritarian relationships between employers and employees. Employees must break free from the autocratic clutches of forced leadership styles and move towards a servant leadership style. The servant leadership style seeks to move management and personnel interaction away from 'controlling activities' toward a more synergistic relationship between both parties.

Greenleaf describes servant leaders as 'leaders who put other people's needs, aspirations and interests above their own. The servant leader's deliberate choice is to serve others. The servant leader's chief motive is to serve first, as opposed to lead. Furthermore, servant leaders seek to help their followers 'grow healthier, wiser, freer, more autonomous, and more likely themselves to become servants.'[47]

Power and authority are double-edged swords; they function as the oppressor and the oppressed. Few successful organizations go beyond the conventional leadership style and practise servant leadership as part of their organizational value. Pursuing the oppressor-oppressed style is socially offensive in the contemporary workforce, hence the need

---

[47]Sendjaya, Sen, and James C. Sarros, 'Servant Leadership: Its Origin, Development, and Application in Organizations', *Journal of Leadership & Organizational Studies*, Vol. 9, No. 2, 2002, pp. 57–58, https://tinyurl.com/82mkcr82, Accessed on 2 June 2025.

for it to be jettisoned. If you are a leader, then you must consciously stop upholding the oppressor-oppressed style and instead work to empower others. Only if you deeply feel the need to liberate yourself can your liberation pave the way for the liberation of the oppressed.

Then, where does one start one's intended psychological liberation? From whom? If you are not haunted by your own feelings and thoughts that you must be free from the destiny to which you are chained, your freedom to work on your passion shall remain a mirage. In that sense, liberation means making career choices which will ensure equity between your personal value creation and well-being, instead of one being upheld at the cost of the other. Building personal value creation (PVC) and well-being (WB) means building mental capital (MC). That is a true path to equilibrium, and therefore liberation.

Path to Equilibrium: Not Selling Your Souls

The path to equilibrium should not be misunderstood as the path of great achievement or achievement at any cost. It is not about building empires on other's ruins, including one's own. It is simply a path to fulfilment. In the single-minded pursuit of achievement, we have constantly disconnected ourselves from the true joy that comes from actualizing our genuine and deepest desires. The process of actualizing is what we need to seek as fulfilment. Too bad, it is often mistaken for achievement.

Words like 'aggressiveness', or terms like 'ultra tech' and 'killer instinct', instantly provoke corporate soldiers to prepare themselves for business battles. What many fail to notice is, this tends to unlock one's primitive coding and trigger subliminal stimuli. Corporate honchos who are conditioned to keep adding more to their coffers are familiar with these words and create a chain of toxicity among their employees. The result is that many employees end up selling their souls, just to achieve. Executives fail to acknowledge that happiness—or is it vanity?—derived from these processes do not last long.

Like an intoxicant, they produce an immediate kick that disappears as quickly as it appeared. On the other hand, fulfilment teaches you to be calm, reduces anxiety, and makes you more human both towards the self and towards others, enabling you to celebrate the experiences with your soul. Metaphorically speaking, achievement is like reading prose; fulfilment is like savouring poetry. While prose is easy to read and understand, poetry aims to touch the inner self and soul, taking on multiple meanings; hence it requires both the mind and the heart. It connects people through passion and love. Fulfilment is internal without a market value that can be put on it.

Fulfilment: Gift unto the Self

Fulfilment is not about what you do for a living, rather why you seek to do it. When I was assigned as an understudy in laboratory (sensitivity) training programmes, the programme facilitator asked us to introduce ourselves the first day. There were several industry bigwigs in the room. The vice president of a reputed company was the first to introduce himself. As he said, 'I am so and so, Vice President, Legal Affairs,' the facilitator retorted by asking, 'Are there any

Vice President, Illegal Affairs, in your company?' And thus the programme began.

Pretty much everyone in the room sensed the sarcasm in the facilitator's question. The VP, who was annoyed at the disrespect meted out to him, had a sort of war of words with the facilitator. Unrelenting and unrepentant, the latter prodded the VP further, asking him if he knew why he had studied law. While the VP went to explain the advantages of studying law his position and its perks, he was again asked the same question. Why had he studied law? Perplexed by the question and irritated by the inability to understand what exactly the facilitator wanted from him, he continued explaining. As he went deeper into his explanation, he spoke of his dreams of helping people and how he felt transported while upholding justice and fairness.

There was a semblance of truce in the voice of the facilitator, and he finally said, 'Now you know why you have chosen law. You may introduce yourself now.' With a sense of pride and acknowledgement of his newfound reasons, the VP introduced himself. Almost like fresh water gushing from a dam, without any trappings of his designation or position. It was indeed a moment of truth and enlightenment for all of us in the room.

During the remaining days of the programme, we didn't have to deal with any designation-related arrogance. The myth of 'what we are' vanished along with our so-called achievements. I must note here, however, that the appropriateness of introducing ourselves as who we are and why we are here depends on the context.

Famed life coach Tony Robbins believes that success

without fulfilment is the ultimate failure.[48] He argues that fulfilment is often mistaken for fame, status, or wealth. Yet if that were truly the case, why do so many accomplished individuals feel desolate or sink into depression? For some, even personal enjoyment becomes a burden, and that discontent tends to affect those around them. In the end, if a person cannot find contentment in who they are or in what they've achieved, that may well be the truest form of failure. Fulfilment is not just making omelettes from eggs. It is the entire process from incubating the eggs till they hatch, and then can be used to make a delicious dish.

You, the Liberator

Liberating the self is dependent on the initiative taken by the self. The criticality of liberating the self lies in the deeper understanding and acceptance of one's conditions of enslavement, of being taken hostage, the corollary being the willingness to liberate the self from the clutches of the 'oppressor' and the commitment to becoming free.

In 2005, the ILO published its second Global Report on Forced Labour under the Declaration of Fundamental Principles and Rights at Work. The Report called for a Global Alliance against Forced Labour, involving governments, workers' and employers' organizations.[49] The

---

[48] Carmody, Bill, 'Tony Robbins: Success Without Fulfilment Is the Ultimate Failure', *Inc.com,* 11 September 2016, https://tinyurl.com/yc4fvr9b. Accessed on 6 May 2025.

[49] 'Business Case Studies on Forced Labour', *International Labour Organization,* 1 August 2010–31 December 2010, https://tinyurl.com/ynknptpk. Accessed on 6 May 2025.

ILO's Special Action Programme to Combat Forced Labour (SAP-FL) subsequently initiated a global initiative to raise awareness of employers' organizations and businesses on modern manifestations of forced labour. To date, a wide range of training and awareness-raising activities have been carried out in close collaboration with the International Organisation of Employers (IOE), while involving major multinational companies and employers' organizations. In 2008, an ILO published a handbook for employers and businesses on combating forced labour, providing guidance on the principles and definitions of forced labour, and the assessment of compliance and action.[50]

The handbook—a booklet on good practice case studies—is largely drawn based on multiple-country experiences. The project aimed to build further on these case studies by studying in greater depth how select companies deal with the risk of forced labour in their own operations and across their supply chains.

The overarching theme was that businesses can and must play a central role in fighting coercive labour practices. The broader aim of the project is to showcase the effective engagement of companies (both multinational enterprises—MNEs—and their suppliers) as they address the challenges that are faced by many companies in the global economy.

ILO considers the following as forced and coercive labour practices:

---

[50]'Combating forced labour: A handbook for employers and business, *International Labour Organization*, revised edition 2015, https://tinyurl.com/mr2hnx2h. Accessed on 6 May 2025.

- Restriction of workers' ability to terminate an employment contract
- Threats of violence and intimidation
- Debt bondage, illegal wage deductions and deception in wage payments
- Sanctions or disciplinary measures that result in an obligation to work or that are used as a punishment for participation in a strike
- Compulsory overtime above the limit permitted in national law and collective agreements
- Restriction of freedom of movement
- Retention of identity documents (against the will of workers and workers not having access to their documents)
- Threats of dismissal and denunciation in the case of irregular migrant workers

Many companies are still engaged in more than one of the aforementioned coercive practices. Executing a bond for a specific number of years and agreeing to work in a particular company is legally untenable in Indian Law. Yet, this practice still continues and regrettably, many employees fall victim to unfair and coerced labour practices.

Being a hostage has a charming side too. It lures people to stay within their comfort zone. The perks that each syndrome offers, encourages them not to exercise other options. A Greenback Cat, whose primary motive is to earn more money, may justify discomforts like excess workload and disruptive family life as a corollary of their choice. We all know that to gain something, we must lose something. While that makes perfect sense, how do we define what we gain and what we lose? Is earning more money at the cost of higher medical bills and sleepless nights considered a meaningful gain? Unfortunately, many of us consciously consent to this predicament.

The decision to lose our peace of mind and well-being arising out of our conscious decision and walking into the hostage situation is the only choice for many hostages by conscience. 'We know the consequences of what we are entering into' is pretty much a self-defeating argument, like a smoker saying I know smoking is injurious to health.

People who claim to be aware of the harmful consequences of being a hostage and who contemplate freedom that has no tangible application remain hostages. Fear looks them in the eye, beckoning them with a toxic cocktail of pragmatism, pessimism and future miseries. Uncertainty about the present and anxiety about the future serve to hold them hostage, while condemning them to a life of stress and tentativeness. While these hostages understand their *whats* and *hows*, they tend to remain ignorant of their *whys*.

Trading the frail present for a possible stronger future appears to be a soft option, a self-inflicted wound, a phantom of our creation. Let us always remember that no one other than we ourselves can free us.

Be Autonomous

Autonomy is about making one's own choices, of one's own volition and being accountable for one's actions and the consequences. Autonomy is self-governed; it enables us to make our own direction. Being autonomous is the fundamental need of an individual. It is the path to self-actualization. Attaining self-actualization has been considered by many to be the pinnacle of life. The Buddha, Nelson Mandela, Mother Teresa—all were self-actualized people. While we are yet to become corporate Buddhas or Mandelas, that should not deter us from seeking our rightful place in the universe.

Our definition of being autonomous is comparatively simple and pragmatic. Be yourself, channelize your passion into your work, and be the master of your own destiny. In a nutshell, let the power to control your actions come from within.

In an unabashed act of recklessness, many of us hand over our internal keys to external factors ranging from physical and material comforts to peer pressure, opinions of others, and even consumerism. In the process, we mortgage our autonomy and social freedom.

No one who is prudent will cut the branch of a tree while sitting on it. That, however, is exactly what we do. With a system and an environment which actively discourage us from being what we want to be, it is doubly hard to be our true selves.

When you lack autonomy, your locus control is hijacked by others who can manipulate you as they wish. The appreciation and disparagement you get are measured by others' yardsticks and not by your expectations, leading to the curtailment of your own strengths, your decision-making and problem-solving capabilities. If you assess yourself through the FIRO-B (Fundamental Interpersonal

Relationship Orientation—Behaviour)[51], a tool created by W. Schutz, it will reveal that your score on the expressed control dimension will be low and the wanted control dimension will be high. That means your comfort level of taking instruction from others and letting them influence and direct you is higher. Obviously, you are not in charge of yourself.

We deprive ourselves of our freedom by choosing not to be autonomous. Haven't we often experienced diminishing autonomy at our workplaces? Faced with these experiences, we are left with more confusion than clarity on what is required of us.

Let me present a hypothetical situation where your superior orders you to do something.

Superior: *You have not kept up your promise and have missed your target for the second time. I don't think you have put in enough effort. No... No, I don't want to know what you do or how you do it. I just want results, starting from next month or get ready to face the consequences.*

---

[51]Fundamental Interpersonal Relations Orientation (FIRO) is a theory of interpersonal relations, introduced by William Schutz in 1958. This theory mainly explains the interpersonal interactions of a group of people. The theory is based on the belief that when people interact/relate in a group, they do so based on three main interpersonal needs—affection/openness, control and inclusion. Schutz developed a measuring instrument that contains six scales of nine-item questions, and this became version B (for 'Behaviour'). This technique was created to measure how group members feel when it comes to affection/openness, control, and inclusion, or to be able to get feedback from people in a group.

While skimming through the above harsh directions, it looks as if the superior neither wanted to understand why his associate was not able to achieve the target, nor was he willing to help the latter with necessary suggestions on how to achieve it. The act is more revealing of the superior's inability to handle the problem effectively and amounts to communicating 'I want results, not you or your feelings.' Though outwardly the associate can make their own decision and improve the result, it becomes amply clear that it doesn't suggest a hopeful way to the 'desired autonomy.' Rather, it is a direction that plunges the associate into greater helplessness—a coerced autonomy, which brings along more pressure and stress as it leaves the associate confused about whether or not they can be truly autonomous.

To become autonomous, one has to align one's thoughts and actions and make rational and appropriate decisions. The outcome of these decisions enables us to become self-assured and helps us tackle our ergophobia. Unfortunately, even in today's changing social milieu, there are not many takers for autonomy since it demands increased responsibilities. Clutching on to others seems like a less stressful option.

After years of being part of HR, my position has obviously demanded making unpopular decisions countless times. At this juncture, I would like to share an incident for its vitality, and especially for underscoring the importance of being assertive and its impact on organizational discipline.

The corporate I was employed at ran a stellar training centre with admirable infrastructure that catered for all group companies. Soon after I joined the company, I was asked to inaugurate a training programme that would begin at 9 a.m. To my dismay, I found only 40 per cent of the participants were present. I was further flustered when they informed me that the remaining participants would join the training programme as and when they could, without indicating the actual time they were likely to come in. The justification for this tardiness was they were all senior managers and could be held up by various more important business-related emergencies. This apathy towards learning, however, was a usual affair and the training sessions just had to go on. While the training team was later admonished about this situation, their helplessness in taming the participants was palpable. They even advised me not to precipitate the issue. I was eventually left with the feeling that the effort, cost, external faculty's image of the company, time and, above all, value of those participants who did come on time didn't seem to be of any importance to the centre.

Being a stickler for punctuality and responsible for the training division, this was obviously unacceptable to me. I approached our president, a charismatic leader whom I reported to, in order to find a solution. We decided that anyone joining later than 5 past 9 would not be able to participate in the programme and this would eventually be relayed to their superiors. So, the training department personnel and other employees of the company and group were notified about this new regulation and were asked to strictly adhere to it.

An uneventful month went by after which we organized a programme for the top management where our president was also a participant. The programme did not begin on time since he did not show up and the participants were anxiously awaiting his arrival. He finally came in after a 12-minute delay only adding to my predicament. My anxiousness apart, I decided to be unbiased and had to tell him to withdraw from the programme, even though most of the vice presidents present were unhappy with my decision. At that point the only thought I had in my mind was, 'I would have done the same to anyone else.'

It so happened, that the president appreciated what I did, and in future meetings, encouraged others to respect learning initiatives, laying stress on how timely participation could go a long way. Needless to say, all future training sessions went through with full and timely attendance.

While telling off the president felt like an immense burden at the time of the incident, the relief that I experienced after carrying out my decision and the benefit it brought to the organization reinforced my belief in being autonomous and assertive. While the preceding experience may seem trivial, its significance was not lost either on me or on several other colleagues.

Being autonomous is a step towards transformation and freedom. Only by inheriting some traits and characteristics can one cherish this world of freedom, where choices are made based upon free will. The essence of free will emerges by treading the symbiotic twin paths, a prerequisite suggested in the chapters that follow. The twin paths provide the hope and strategies for liberation and a life of inner peace.

9

The Paths to Liberation

The Buddha propounded the Four Noble Truths and the Eightfold Path to liberation through his sermons. The Eightfold Path is holistic and easy to embrace. Yet, only a few follow it mindfully in order to end their suffering. The essence of the path to liberation stems from our mind, and how we tune it.

Inspired by certain teachings of the Buddha, I wanted to experience becoming mindful and self-aware. So I travelled abroad and stayed in a few Buddhist monasteries. I had life-altering experiences during my stays which made me aware of my own frailty. No one expressly taught me anything in the monasteries but I had a few insights merely by being in such spaces. I realized how a simple change of habit could transform many dimensions of my life. Take for instance my food habits. Though I was not a gourmand, the absence of certain ingredients from food drove me round the bend. But this unwanted need faded away after experiencing the following episode.

Traditionally Buddhist monks do not cook food; they depend on food received from others as alms. On any given day, three or more donors would wait to offer food. All monks and other inmates would sit in a row with a wooden bowl in hand. The donors would serve different dishes—oats porridge, bread and jam, rice with curry and vegetables, etc.—in the monks' bowls, but one immediately after another. When I was served the same way, I wondered how to eat the food that was all mixed up, reflecting a momentary conflict between my pleasure principle and my immediate context. While I ate with a certain amount of distaste, I observed how the monks were eating mindfully, with gratitude. At that moment, I decided to give up my fondness for ideal cooking and ideal food. While this may seem like a simple example, yet it became a milestone in my life! My perspective about many things in life changed. Now, I actively practice zero fondness for material things, external appreciation and approval, among others—indeed a true liberation for me.

Wherever I deliver a talk on the Buddha's Four Noble Truths and Eightfold Path to liberation, people ask me whether it is possible to uncover one's Buddha nature in a hostile environment and ecosystem such as ours? The reality of the environment and the ecosystem notwithstanding, I respond with the borrowed wisdom of the Buddha's Noble Middle Path—a metaphor for a balanced life. Tuning a string too tight can make it snap, while tuning it too loose produces no sound at all. This understanding can be applied in various spheres of our life. If we resolve to follow this path of direction, purpose and meaning dedicatedly, we are on the path to liberation!

This chapter aims to present the eightfold path for people's liberation from the hostage syndrome by categorizing them under two broad themes: 1) personal value creation (Paths 1–4) and 2) well-being (Paths 5–8).

Following all these paths may be tough, but you could pick a few, which could eventually motivate you to follow the rest. As long as people see life through the light of awareness, they will become enlightened, like lighting a candle in their life to illuminate it, to drive away their darkness and to give warmth to them and to others.

Personal Value Creation

Personal value (PV) can be defined as a set of distinct behavioural patterns and characteristics that create special value in life, be it at work, in society or in the family. In other words, PV amalgamates 'who I am, what I do, and a personal reflection on myself.' It radiates one's personal credibility and makes the world respond to us as we are.

In the corporate context, personal values determine our entry in and exit from an organization. To build these values (if not done already), you must probe and assess yourself to find how much value you have been able to add in your personal value creation (PVC). Are you a resolute and dedicated executive willing to build those values to enhance your value quotient?

Path I: Being Self-Aware

Self-awareness is commonly used in all developmental lexicon, personal effectiveness training and self-help books. While it appears to be the latest buzzword, it has in fact been around for centuries. Ancient philosophers and sages across the world, including the Buddha have always taught the importance of self-awareness—a concept easily thrown around but probably among the most difficult to comprehend and follow. Being self-aware implies deep reflection and I have hypothesized that it starts with our thinking and feeling. Being cognizant of self-awareness is one thing, and integrating it into our daily lives is quite another thing. Time and again researchers have proven that there is a glaring gap between the science of self-awareness and the art of walking the talk.

Self-awareness results from the constant practice of being in touch with the self. It is worth noting that constant practice alone opens the gates to self-awareness and helps us connect with our true emotional and mental states. Our decisions, communications and relationships would be more harmonious if we were more self-aware. Our inability to handle high-stress situations, our sudden emotional outbursts can all be attributed to a fundamental lack of self-awareness. Our behaviour as an employee, a leader or even a parent is governed by the effectiveness of our self-awareness.

Unfortunately, despite its importance, self-awareness has still not been given its due importance as a critical life skill. Our narcissistic attitude, and inertia in cultivating self-awareness, deprives us from reaping its benefits. While introspection is important, it isn't enough to yield the results of constant practice of self-awareness.

Dr Tasha Eurich, an organizational psychologist, researcher, and a *New York Times* bestselling author, says that while introspection is commonly believed to enhance self-awareness, her research shows it often has the opposite effect of reducing self-awareness and overall well-being. This is primarily because most people introspect incorrectly, especially by asking 'why' questions. These questions aim to uncover unconscious motives, but since such motives are largely inaccessible, individuals often create inaccurate explanations. As a result, they may misinterpret their thoughts and behaviours, leading to flawed self-assessments and poor decision making.[52]

I value and concur with Dr Eurich's point of view. Most performance appraisals reveal this gap. When a manager discusses a subordinate's performance but offers limited or no financial benefit or promotion opportunities, the discussion often results in silence or an emotional outburst.

In my experience in HR, both the appraiser and appraisee act guarded or unguarded based on their expectations of the outcome. These discussions are frequently overshadowed by scepticism and a lack of transparency, often creating a tense atmosphere.

I believe it would be beneficial if appraisers approached these discussions with empathy, supported by objective data and evidence; this could make the appraisee more receptive. Similarly, if appraisees present data and evidence of their performance, appraisers might be more transparent, leading to more meaningful discussions.

However, many discussions conclude without significant learning because emotions can overwhelm self-awareness. Both the appraiser and appraise focus on what

---

[52]Eurich, Tasha, 'What Self-Awareness Really Is (and How to Cultivate It)', *Harvard Business Review*, 4 January 2018, https://tinyurl.com/mpar8me6. Accessed on 6 May 2025.

and who—they tend to miss the 'why'. While individuals might believe they 'know who they are', genuine self-awareness is a distinct concept. Knowing oneself and being self-aware are two different things. I do not suggest doing away with introspection, but only pruning it to be effective. Here is a (really) short story to illustrate more succinctly the aforementioned points.

> *A horse suddenly came galloping down the road. It seemed as though the man on the horse had somewhere important to go. Another man, who was standing on the roadside, shouted, 'Where are you going?'*
>
> *The man on the horse replied, 'I don't know! Ask the horse!'*

While several interpretations and explanations can be given for this story, the interpretation I personally like is that of the horse symbolizing our energy. The story focuses on how we usually live our lives—at the mercy of our habits that are normally formed not by our own deep-seated desires and intentional actions, but rather by our surroundings and mindless activities.

The path to self-awareness is not trouble-free. From time to time, if we stopped to ask ourselves why exactly we run around so much, we might find an answer, albeit not a very comforting one. We are used to 'running around' since that's how we are taught to live. Unfortunately, the more we run, the more it gets us nowhere. We need to learn how to take back the reins and let the horse know who the master is. We are, and have always been the master, so let's start behaving like one!

Path II: Challenge Your Mental Models

Mental models can be construed as the fulcrum of our thinking. They help our understanding of people and situations and help us make appropriate decisions. They are framed by and through our past experiences and introjections (unconscious adoption of unverified attitudes of others). However, these models are not always error-free. To give an example, elders are often considered to be wise. While this is a general statement, it is not always true.

We carry similar mental models when it comes to dealing with the self and others, at work and in our personal relationships. Many a time, these models remain and operate from our subconscious mind with outcomes that are either rewarding or devastating. Despite our experiences we allow ourselves to remain rigid without challenging these mental models. This could be partly due to the few favourable and immediate results we may have had.

Another example of a rigid and prevalent mental model commonly used by many is that business and ethics do not go hand in hand. These frameworks consist of underlying assumptions strung together by values, beliefs and experiences—both of ourselves and that of others. They simply mirror how we understand our world and how that understanding eventually dictates our actions.

One of the contemporary mental models creating confusion and chaos among millennials and other young executives is 'the longer the stay in a company, the lesser the market value.' We have discussed in detail the effects and defects of mobility in Chapter 4: Types of Hostage Syndromes.

Multiple questions arise at this point. Should we change our existing mental models? If so, why? This would often depend on our answer to another panoptic question: Is change an option or a compulsion? Change as an option ideally arises from the progressive and holistic outlook one has, whereas compulsion simply arises from a crisis. What many of us fail to understand is that we are in a crisis.

One of my clients approached me for help with his daughter's employment. She had been struggling for a year to land a job despite being an MBA graduate. While her desperation was clear to me, I realized she had neither the confidence nor any specific skill set required for a job. I understood her father did not allow her to gain any experiences of her own. He seemed immensely protective of her but anxious as well that she should have a job. His innocence and ignorance pushed him to the point of saying he would take her every day to the workplace if she landed a job. What was shocking however was when he quipped that she only needed to be employed until her marriage, as her husband would then be able to take care of her.

Any psychologist would immediately think of several ways to analyse this case. I prefer to confine this only to the mental model concept to further the discussion on the topic. The father in question strongly believed his daughter was incapable of doing anything on her own. If you analyse this further, you would be able to understand his perception of women in general too. While his daughter was aware of her father's prejudices, his protective nature and even her own victimhood, she was not inclined not to challenge his mental model. Getting a job was an imperative for her and her father, since that would facilitate the process leading up to her marriage. Of course, the above case is set in the Indian context, where the chances for working women to get married is brighter.

Unless people think there is a real need to change, it may be difficult to help them realize that their mental models need to be challenged. As goes the famous quote widely attributed to Einstein, 'It is insanity to do the same things repeatedly expecting a different result.'

When playing a match, the attitude of 'I should not lose' may not yield the same result as 'I ought to win.' Each model can influence the outcome differently. Our decisions and strategies are driven by our thinking and this influences our information gathering, how we use that information and how we deploy our resources to achieve what we aim to. The barrier we face when challenging our mental models is our unwillingness to change. Since these models not only influence our reasoning and behaviour but also our transactional outcomes, it is imperative to embrace change.

Challenging our beliefs and assumptions is never a cakewalk, but it can give rise to the awareness of the need to change. Unless we become self-aware, we tend to do things in the same way.

Question Your Assumptions

Questioning our status quo is the first step towards changing our mental model. This would be the starting point for any developmental journey. A starting point has no locked doors. For those who believe it does, all you need to do is push hard, and you will find the doors were never locked in the first place.

A personal experience about thirty-five years ago will help you see how mental models can impede us from making new and innovative decisions. During my tenure at a 5-star hotel in Bengaluru, the F&B department planned to conduct a food festival and a meeting was convened to discuss various issues, including introducing new dishes in the menu. The meeting was attended by all HODs and chefs. A trainee chef put forth an idea which was unheard of at that time (mid-eighties), 'Let us introduce fried ice cream,' he said. Obviously, many people gawked at the suggestion. Surprisingly, the F&B manager too shot down the idea, asserting ice cream should only be served cold. While the majority of the crowd agreed with the F&B manager, the trainee chef still tried to convince everyone. At this point, the general manager stepped in and asked about the recipe and how it would be served. As the trainee chef provided a list of ingredients which seemed odd and mismatched (eggs, cornflakes and ice cream), he explained the process of making it as well. Luck proved to be on his side as the general manager seconded his idea, and fried ice cream turned out to be a huge hit with the customers at the festival.

In our subsequent review meeting, the trainee chef was rightfully rewarded and the rest were censured for their conventionality and the ridicule with which they initially handled the situation. Only on further reflection did I understand how a rigid mental model of how ice cream should be eaten/served needed to be opened up to other innovative possibilities. Thus, this episode only serves to underscore that innovation is the foundation of product development and product differentiation.

Only an open, enquiring mind can steer any developmental process effectively. An 'I don't know yet' attitude acts as a fertile ground for seeding change. In martial arts, *'mushin'* or 'the mind without mind' is a strategy or mental state that teaches you to be free of any prejudices or thoughts, thus liberating your mind to being open to everything. While the concept itself merits a larger discussion, essentially having an open mind and questioning assumptions will enable us to achieve the difference we hope to.

Once an engineer, as directed by his company, came to see me. This young man had twelve years of professional experience in a mid-sized company and was known for his positive business attitude and technical expertise. His bosses never complained about his work or his people skills, but made a mention of his poor risk-taking attitude when faced with the challenge of taking on greater responsibilities. The management decided to send him for a short-term course in business management toa premier institution in Singapore. To their dismay, he abandoned the course halfway and returned to India intending to put in his papers. Shocked and perplexed by his actions, the management sought reasons for his decision. He could only come up with a single reason that led to his final decision to quit—'personal'. Luckily, his considerate management sent him over to me to seek professional advice.

After two sessions with him, I concluded that while he was grateful to his company and to his superiors for the opportunity, he felt that he would let them down if they expected him to take on more responsibilities once his course was completed in Singapore. His fear of failure, loss of good name, and maybe even the job, stopped him from completing the course. I confronted him by asking, 'If the job is so important, why do you want to resign?' He replied that it was an emotional decision. When I delved deeper, he revealed what was plaguing him: 'What will others think of me if I fail?'

Do we have to allow our assumptions of others to overshadow our potential? Is it a constructive, meaningful trade-off? Let's aim to shake off this yoke and celebrate our potential. Challenging one's assumption paves the path to change.

Reseeding

Effecting a paradigm shift is similar to uprooting and replanting a tree. Digging deep into the existing mindset precedes the 'reseeding'. Unless one engages in a reflective dialogue with the self, reseeding will simply be a fragmented, fruitless process. A change in status quo means disturbing and disrupting the self, the system, the structure and others. One needs to be prepared to venture beyond the comfort zone, an upsetting factor and a cause for resistance for many. Experiencing conflicts is inherent to this process and may frustrate you to the point where this may push you either back to where you had started or probably propel you to where you have never been.

Organizations breed certain mental models which ought to be challenged in order to bring about greater effectiveness. Many have tried and many still want to try, yet the steps taken to this end are largely derailed by the complexity of such a process and the self-doubt many harbour about its execution.

The key to progress in the developmental journey of the self or the organization, is knowing who you are and who you think you ought to be. Once the gap between the two is understood, the process of watering the seed becomes meaningful and easy.

To think I am right (always) is not right. Persisting with this mental model not only clouds our cognitive faculties but also displays our arrogance. A big stumbling block in our learning curve is maintaining our life's position on the auto mode of—I am okay and you are not okay. Accumulation of knowledge alone cannot be equated with development.

To learn, one must begin to unlearn!

Path III: Build Personal Values

Leaders who steal credit for their team's good work, let alone appreciate them, cannot be regarded as trustworthy. Such leaders often have a low credibility quotient. Undoubtedly, value-starved individuals display this kind of self-serving attitude. What is such a leader's value for the team members who only have this leader to look up to?

Values, Defined

Personal values are the core that defines who we are. They are formed and influenced by our cultural conditioning, personal experiences, and the wisdom of our understanding within the family and outside. To arrive at an easy definition of values is impossible as various research papers suggest different definitions. Researchers themselves have had difficulty agreeing on what values mean and how we understand them. With due respect to researchers and scholars who study values as their subject matter, I have hypothesized a simple interpretation of what value means for our understanding and for the sake of this discussion.

Values stem from our beliefs and have the potential to influence our ongoing internal and external transactions. Equality, honesty, punctuality and integrity are all examples of core values that we uphold every day. Values exercise a major influence on human behaviour and attitude and collectively serve as a guide in most situations. Leading one's life while abiding by these values can present countless challenges and can affect their personal ecosystem and practice. Articulating truthfulness everywhere may bring challenges.

Let's imagine that while you are seeking a new job for your career growth, a multinational startup offers you a suitable position. After accepting the offer, you are tipped to join as head of HR which comes with a hefty pay package, perks and also responsibilities which you seem to enjoy.

After joining, you realize that the company is contemplating exploiting the project affected people (PAP)[53] of the local community by violating certain clauses

[53]Projected affected people (PAP): Any person(s) who, on account of the execution of the project, or any of its components or sub-projects or parts thereof, would have their (i) right, title or interest in any house, land (including residential, agricultural and grazing land) or any other fixed or moveable asset acquired or possessed, in full or in part, permanently

of the agreement that was entered into when the latter parted with their land. One clause in particular states unambiguously that the company will offer the cost of the land and a job to one adult in the family (subject to certain conditions). However, you realize, not only is the company trying to violate certain clauses, it is also diluting some of the conditions specified especially with regard to offering a job to the PAP. What is worse is—the company expects you to spearhead this assignment.

Your values, honesty and loyalty encourage you to have a sensible dialogue with the top management, but everything you say falls on deaf ears. At the end of your tether, you consider quitting since putting up with this corporate culture is anathema to you and doesn't fit in your value system.

There could be multiple ways of handling such a situation. You would be the best judge in these circumstances, and how you would or could handle the situation would be based on your values. However, defining these values and implementing them may not be simple. Building a value system and practising the same is a choice left to us. The meaning and intensity will vary depending on the importance given to the context or to ourselves.

---

or temporarily; or (ii) business, occupation, work, place of residence or habitat adversely affected; or (iii)standard of living adversely affected. Development Bank of the Philippines, and Frank Radstake. *Philippines – Second Local Government Units (LGU) Urban Water Supply and Sanitation Project: Resettlement Action Plan. Vol. 1: Policy Framework on Involuntary Resettlement and Compensation for Land and Assets.* Development Bank of the Philippines, 2005. https://tinyurl.com/25kejwxn. Accessed on 6 May 2025.

I have experienced three types of people based on their value systems: value centerers, value dissenters, and value shallowers.

Value 'centerers' figure in the top layer of Maslow's hierarchy principles.[54] If they are asked to choose between material things or principles, they cling to the latter. Perhaps they may be labelled as rigid, unrealistic and alien in today's context. Yet, this species takes on the burden of spreading fairness, equality and justice among us. Be it punctuality or having an unblemished track record of financial dealings or upholding and choosing humanistic values over other things, for a value centerer, values cannot be graded into important and unimportant.

Value 'dissenters' are generally self-centred people who consider values to be real barriers for their growth. They tend to be mavericks and are go-getters. Perhaps, not surprisingly enough, many organizations encourage them to be part of their growth. Value dissenters thrive on the maxim 'be flexible and move on.' Justifying their unethical practices or being indifferent to values doesn't make them the least bit uncomfortable. Psychologically, their internal anger and frustration against the world for being unkind to them could be a probable cause. However, their tendency to be insensitive continues to push them into quagmires.

Value 'shallowers' are very fluid and generally go with the flow. They do not have any serious opinion on issues that are contentious; they are quite unpredictable when it

---

[54]Maslow, Abraham H., 'A theory of human motivation,' *Psychological Review*, Vol. 50, No. 4, 1943, pp. 370–396, https://tinyurl.com/2htuwmwt. Accessed on 30 May 2025.

comes to value-oriented decisions and they resist getting drawn into any introspective or self-reflective process. Often without realizing, they enjoy themselves at the cost of others' pain, but a bit of shaking up their psychological moorings could help them refocus on their values.

Value conflicts: Such conflicts can erupt in the workplace anytime. On a comparative note, I can safely assume that when value centerers make decisions, they face far less value conflicts as they are value-centred. Value dissenters hardly face situations of conflict by virtue of their scarcity of values. And the experiences of value shallowers would be varied due to their shifting beliefs. Making value-based decisions in an organization, depending on the intensity and nature of the consequences is always tough. That said, these assumptions are based on my experiences only and would need to be explored further using appropriate research techniques for greater validation.

Let's revisit the example of the HR head who is aware of the company's exploitation of the PAPs, and see how each of the above value categories approaches this conflict.

Approach of value centerers

They understand that the issue is contrary to their values, hence the action will be broadly based on the following choices:

- They can make the management aware of the consequences of the violation and advise them not to proceed further.
- If the management doesn't agree with their line of

thinking, it may request the management to take such a manger off that particular assignment.

- They may quit as such a practice is unacceptable to their value system.

Approach of value dissenters

- They understand the needs of the company and facilitate the assignment by getting involved in it.
- They remain insensitive to values and ethics.
- They value the company's and their personal interest over the unfairness meted out to the PAPs.

Approach of value shallowers

- They are indecisive due to lack of a sure value system.
- They are inclined to lean on the opinion of the majority and be influenced by others' emotional appeal.
- Their tentativeness and fear of losing their job determine their decision.

Internal value conflicts can often occur due to clashes in our own value systems. Values can be situational, hierarchical and subjective. (If a few of the PAPs are relatives or friends of the value shallowers, their decision may be different.) Many of our values are challenged on a daily basis. However, as we develop inner maturity through our personal experiences, we will have the ability to live by certain unwavering values, no matter the situation. These will eventually become our 'core values'.

Cognitive psychology deems our core values as something that run deeper than our beliefs—at a subconscious level. Knowing our true values is crucial to our happiness. While values are varied, core values are absolute; they seldom change and they are principle-centric. Their supremacy over peripheral values in the journey of life remains unequivocal. For example, loyalty may be a core value for a company whereas quality of performance can be considered a peripheral value. Core and peripheral values are interchangeable and are particular to each company's work culture and vision. A life oblivious to core values will certainly lead to anxiety, tentativeness and may disturb one's existence. This is valid as much for an individual as for an organization.

The sheer number of executives who are enslaved by their own ignorance and insensitive about value clarification is astounding. I often find myself in disagreements with clients due to value conflicts during my consultancy assignments.

Once, an auto ancillary company engaged me to develop second line leaders. The company was well known for practising its unwritten but non-negotiable culture of loyalty. The company consciously institutionalized loyalty as the core value among its employees which transformed progressively into their culture. Eighty per cent of the employees were either from the same community/religion as the owners or were referred by existing employees. The management still claims that their success is basically due to their employees' loyalty.

On working closely with the employees, I realized

their slave mentality, and their inability to escape from this timidity has contributed significantly to their so-called loyalty. The entire assignment was an irony of sorts; developing effective second line leaders while all the top line leaders still believed in, professed and practised loyalty to their owners. Among the people I interacted with, many were symbolically deaf and dumb. Their suspicion and unwillingness to open up, even to each other, almost made it seem like they were frightened. They believed being expressive would create problems in their workspace. It was quite obvious that their family lives were non-existent as work demanded them to put in extra hours as well.

So what happens when we live a life that's not true to our values? A one-word answer could be 'unhappiness'. What is the worst that can happen to anyone besides masking unhappiness and pretending to be happy. There will never be a true self and as long as people are constantly manipulated, driven by anxiety and live like underdogs.

Being happy is a choice and we can make that choice if we identify and clarify our core values. Irrespective of where and how our core values are used, I believe they have the following common features:

- Enduring
- Unchanging; unwavering
- Intrinsic
- Principle-centric
- Hardly negotiable

Path IV: Be Decisive

If work is a house, then decisions are the keys to its locks. Irrespective of hierarchy, everyone has to make decisions. Anyone who practises and resides in a house of indecisiveness hardly emerges a leader either in an organization or elsewhere. Why then are people in the lower rung made to believe that decision making should be the prerogative of those higher up? Are they not, by their own practice, yielding to and obeying the mighty and in many ways partaking in forms of neo-slavery?

Hostages have to think and make certain decisions if they want to escape from captivity. In our life and in our career, we would like to associate with those who make decisions, provide direction and offer support. We like them because they are decisive, regardless of whether their decisions are right or wrong. Very few who have mastered the art of being decisive, use indecisiveness as a strategy. The indecisiveness that I speak of here, is postponing decision-making for certain valid reasons. This cannot be construed as inaction. The animal kingdom is the best example for strategic decisiveness regarding both time and space. Both the hunter and the hunted have to run for their existence, with frequent role reversals as dictated by the desire for survival.

Likewise, one has to act. Poor risk taking, over-analysis of consequences and the unwillingness to lose existing comforts tend to turn people into flip-floppers. An old story, to sharpen thinking and hone decision-making capabilities, one that can be shared with adults and children alike, comes to mind.

A group of children were playing near two railway tracks, one still in use while the other disused. Only one child played on the disused track, the rest on the operational track.

The train is coming, and you are just beside the track interchange. You can make the train change its course to the disused track and save most of the kids[55]*.*

However, that would also mean the lone child playing by the disused track would be sacrificed.

Or would you rather let the train go its way?

Let's take a pause to think about what kind of decision we could make... Most people might choose to divert the course of the train and sacrifice only one child. You might think the same way, I guess. Exactly, I thought the same way initially because to save most of the children at the expense of only one child was a rational decision most people would make, morally and emotionally.

But, have you ever thought that the child choosing to play on the disused track had in fact made the right decision to play at a safe place? Nevertheless, he had to be sacrificed because of his ignorant friends who chose to play where the danger was.

This kind of dilemma happens around us every day. In the office, community, in politics, and especially in a democratic society, the minority is often sacrificed for the interest of the majority, no matter how foolish or ignorant the majority are, and how farsighted and

---

[55]Bharadwaj, Deepa, 'Navigating Tough Choices: Would You Divert the Train?,' *CiteHR*, https://tinyurl.com/y7ek3nrc. Accessed on 14 October 2025.

knowledgeable the minority are. The child who chose not to play with the rest on the operational track was sidelined. And in case he was sacrificed, no one would shed a tear for him.

When we are faced with a similar situation, how many of us decide to stay back and help the children? How many of us let the train continue on its course? Obviously, many of us prefer to run away from tough situations due to our own fears of being incapable of facing challenges, and would love to avoid tackling dangerous situations. This story is primarily for them. I am sure they would be familiar with this kind of a situation.

The great critic Leo Velski Julian who told the story said he would not try to change the course of the train because he believed that the kids playing on the operational track should have known very well that track was still in use, and that they would have run away if they heard the train's sirens. If the train was diverted, that lone child would definitely die because he never thought the train could come over to that track! Moreover, that track was not in use probably because it was not safe. If the train was diverted to the track, we could put the lives of all passengers on board at stake! And in your attempt to save a few kids by sacrificing one child, you might end up sacrificing hundreds of people to save these few kids.

Moving away from the hypothetical situation, let's get back to reality.

While we are all aware that life is full of tough decisions that need to be made, we may not realize that hasty decisions may not always be the right one.

'Remember that what's right isn't always popular... and what's popular isn't always right.'

Everybody makes mistakes; that's why they put erasers on pencils.

Effective decision making is an art. The art of balancing one's left and right brain is something that cannot be mastered instantaneously. Being sensitive about the context and the consequences is as vital as the core values and customs/culture of the environment. An effective decision maker weighs the hurdles and challenges ahead and the complexity of the issues and problems. Practising, learning, unlearning and practising again will hone that skill, which will ultimately be transformed into an art. All of us have encountered and made decisions on questions such as: *How does one choose one's career? Do I want to be an automobile engineer or a journalist? Or do I want to be an automobile engineer and a journalist? How do you make a decision when an employer of your company recommends a candidate to be on board whom you consider unsuitable?* Perhaps the questions may have been different for different people, but the dilemma while taking a decision on them, remains quite similar.

To make your PVC stronger, being decisive is not a choice; it is mandatory. Also, how do we know our PVC is working? Feedback! That is critical. 'Take the time to get feedback from your clients, co-workers, boss, family, whomever,' many noted organizational consultants have concurred. Wise people will listen to the feedback willingly. All the three elements (listening-feedback-willingly) are crucial for building a quality life. Practise! Then practise some more!

Well-Being

Lack of clarity about our goals, values and intentions is detrimental to our well-being (WB). We often skim over the word 'well-being' without paying much attention and use it as a synonym for good health, especially when we offer advice to others.

Living in an era of rapid innovations and a knowledge-dominated economy, we tend to use our heads more than our hearts; the results are pretty evident. The criticality of mental health is overpowering that of physical health. Consequently, the former has become an important economic factor for the working class. Distress signals are plenteous when it comes to work-related stress, burnout, depression and a plethora of mental health problems. The enormous costs associated with them, in terms of reduced productivity, increased absenteeism and work disability, result in reduced human capital investment and increased health care costs. Despite mental health being an important issue, managers—inevitably caught in a Catch-22 position—are seldom able to do much to address such matters.

Well-being primarily consists of one's psychological and physical state that are always interrelated. Human beings are often trapped in the false belief that money and material may fetch this 'well-being'. Reality proves otherwise. It would be redundant for me to substantiate this with evidence and data. I am sure most of us are aware of what I intend to communicate at this juncture. Personally, money and material wealth are not sources of well-being for me, but I do see them as concomitant perks. They do not deserve to be in command of our life, nor must we let our lives be 'defined' by them, as that would undoubtedly lead to emotional deprivation and loss of equilibrium.

Mental Capital and Well-Being
The Government Office for Science (GO-Science) in London, set up a project named 'Foresight Mental Capital and Wellbeing Project (2008)'[56] to advise the government and the private sector on how to achieve the best possible mental development and well-being for everyone in the UK. This project was intended for policy-makers and a wide range of professionals and researchers whose interests related to mental capital and well-being. The report focuses on the UK but in my view, may also be relevant for other countries. The project sought to generate an understanding of the science of mental capital and well-being and a vision of the size and nature of future challenges. Analysis of strategic options for addressing future challenges were conducted and an action plan developed. For background, the project drew upon current research and commissioned reviews of the state-of-the-art science in medicine, biology, psychiatry, psychology, technology and social sciences.

[56]'Foresight Mental Capital and Wellbeing Project: Final Project Report', 2008, Government Office for Science, https://tinyurl.com/38y32dxe. Accessed on 6 May 2025.

Mental capital is defined in that project research paper as 'the totality of an individual's cognitive and emotional resources', and mental well-being as 'a dynamic state in which the individual is able to develop their potential, work productively [...] build positive relationships [...] and contribute to their community.'[57]

Mental capital is likened to financial stock that can be nurtured and accumulated throughout life, but that also experiences highs and lows during its entire trajectory. Mental well-being facilitates optimal and judicious use of the capital so that it is not depleted. The papers in the volume detail the best available evidence of how best to nurture and accumulate mental capital at the level of the individual and the community, and how to put these to judicious use, mindful of the existing and likely future challenges (i.e. drivers of change; e.g. an ageing population, technological innovations in the workplace, immigration, changes in the physical environment, global burden of depression, among others). Five broad areas are subsumed under mental capital and well-being:

1. Mental capital and well-being throughout life
2. Learning through life
3. Mental health and ill health
4. Well-being and work
5. Intellectual disabilities

[57]'Foresight Mental Capital and Wellbeing Project: Executive Summary', 2008, Government Office for Science, p. 10, https://tinyurl.com/37zz5uyw. Accessed on 6 May 2025.

The report seeks to provide a road map for how society can optimally harness the creativity and mental capacities of its individual members if they (countries and persons) are to be competitive in the globalized, technology- and market-driven world of the twenty-first century. This excellent collection of papers was put together to inform policy and practice at the levels of government, industry, academia, and professions related to medicine, health and the social sciences.

This study underscores the importance of revisiting our psychological well-being and understanding how much of it is being used and abused to fulfil our insatiable thirst for material wealth. I would invite the readers to go through this collection and to seek answers for the following fundamental queries:

- Are we sensitized enough about the importance of our own well-being?
- Are we trading our well-being for material wealth and in the process becoming eternal hostages?
- Do we strive to create an ambience where we are able to contribute to our own well-being and the well-being of our family, our community?

The most important factors for our well-being are:

- Family and work-life balance
- Decreased stress
- Good health
- Inner harmony and peace

These are not standalone factors; each leads to the other almost hierarchically, and eventually leads to inner harmony and peace—the only path to our well-being!

'Amma, can you stay back home at least today?' A six-year-old girl asks her mother.

The guilt-ridden mother turns her head the other way to ensure the child does not see her tear-filled eyes, says sorry and leaves for work.

In most family counselling sessions, a standard statement I hear, especially from adolescents, is: 'My father doesn't even know me.' At times parents have even rebuked their children, stating heartlessly that they should appreciate the former's predicament since *their job 'needs' them.*

Covid-19 added an entirely new dimension to the issue of work-life balance. The unpredictability induced by the pandemic and the subsequent lockdowns compelled people to focus not only on their loved ones' well-being, but on their own life too. This is evident from an anxious and frightened son's concern about his mother—a nurse in a hospital where she was quarantined: 'Will my mother return home safe? And when?!'

In the post-Covid era or otherwise, due to moral turpitude, inept actions and insignificant consequences, several parents find themselves in a dilemma and inevitably end up asking themselves: *What the hell are we doing with our lives?*

Reactions to this question are varied. Some redraw their career plans in order to accommodate the existing needs of their family and children, while others continue to immerse themselves in their day-to-day work transactions, sealing all possibilities of liberation.

What makes an average Indian's work-life balance seem

like a page from Dante's *Inferno*? There are more than nine circles of hell one has to cross! Work-life balance is no longer a topic of discussion confined to just training rooms and seminars. It is time to put it into practice. The input-output ratio of working hours to time spent on one's personal as well as family's well-being should provide food for thought.

An essential yet often overlooked aspect for achieving a sustainable work-life balance is one's place of residence. In India, most major cities are densely populated, with failing infrastructure, and increasingly inhospitable living conditions. The relentless pace, poor civic amenities, and long commutes chip away at whatever time and energy people might otherwise have to devote to their family or to themselves. In such an environment, how does one even begin to talk about well-being or work-life balance? When the very spaces people call home become a source of exhaustion rather than renewal, the idea of meaningful balance starts to feel out of reach.

The Arcadis Sustainable Cities Index 2024, ranks hundred global cities on four parameters of sustainability: people, planet, profit and progress. These represent social, environmental, economic and transformative sustainability and offer an indicative picture of the health and wealth of cities for the present and the future. The research shows that cities across the world are not effectively balancing these four pillars of sustainability. Instead, many demonstrate split personalities. While taking the lead in some areas, cities often underperform in one or other area(s) of sustainability which negatively impacts their overall performance.

European cities dominate the overall ranking.

Amsterdam leads the overall cities ranking and tops the planet sub-index. But, while it scores high in profit, it reveals its split personality by appearing in the forty-fourth place for people. Indian cities are far behind in the overall index of sustainability: Kolkata ranks ninety-one, Hyderabad eighty-eight, Bengaluru eighty-seven and Delhi eighty-five out of hundred.[58] This gives a fair idea of the likely ranks of other Indian cities!

Work-life balance doesn't mean that one has to spend equal time, mathematically speaking, in both places. That is neither practical nor rational. Jim Bird, Founder of worklifebalance.com, and speaker, says there is no one-size-fits-all approach and/or solution for this issue.[59] I concur; though I prefer to see family and work both as an integral part of life rather than work vs family. Both are interdependent, but should not come at the cost of each other. However, it is important to work out the work-life balance effectively, keeping in mind the following factors:

- Monetary capability to meet one's basic needs
- Fulfilment in one's career
- Quality time with family members

The equation between these three factors, needs to be defined individually since each one's needs and definition of these factors are different.

---

[58]Arcadis, '2,000 Days to Achieve a Sustainable Future', *The Arcadis Sustainable Cities Index2024*, https://tinyurl.com/4u6je8jc. Accessed on 5 June 2025.

[59]Bird, Jim, 'Work-Life Balance Defined', *worklifebalance.com*, https://tinyurl.com/4p27nwj8. Accessed on 5 June 2025.

Money and Needs

What may seem a decent amount of money to one, may not be the same to another. A close look at this statement will help us understand its meaning. There are many reasons quoted throughout this book as to why a person chases money. However, one of the prime reasons that must be mentioned in order to provoke some thought is actually *not knowing the reason* for doing so.

Why do we consider money to be everything? The standard responses for this question include that it is indispensable, that one simply cannot live without it, that it determines our lifestyle and comfort level, to name a few. These shallow answers stop us from delving into the actual reason. If we did, we would know for sure that money really isn't everything and it cannot purchase most of the basics that we require for our well-being.

We have been led to believe in the power of money, and have thereby created a state where more money facilitates more power. Money has been known to safeguard people against the vagaries of lives. However, chasing money for the sake of power, superiority, amassing wealth for future generations, and other shallow reasons can never guarantee creating a sense of well-being and peace either among ourselves or within.

Covid has taught many people that money is not the main reason for happiness. This has been backed by research studies. The churning caused by the certainty of impermanence during the Covid pandemic has altered the way we look at work-life balance. The pandemic has pushed almost everyone to work from home with mixed results/experiences.

Most people expected that working from home would be beneficial to them; they believed they could take care of their families better. Unfortunately for many, the constant physical presence at home has had a more negative impact than positive. The line between office hours and family hours was blurred and, in many cases, wiped out completely, with several people working more than fifteen hours a day. This has in turn caused more burnouts and acrimony between spouses, ruined families and relationships, especially in cases where both partners were working. Living in the world of virtual reality, the woes of women multiplied as their domestic responsibilities increased. The end result was that people's well-being was compromised. A change of work location provided a better work-life balance, which many had neither understood nor experienced before. While many organizations identified this as a strategy to retain good performers, both employees and employers need to understand that a mere exchange of location and time for work without a focus on productivity can lead to non-productive environment for both.

Ricardo Semler, in his book *The Seven Day Weekend: Changing the Way Work Works* (2003), says companies have to put employee freedom and satisfaction ahead of corporate goals. He promotes the idea of a company where employees need not follow fixed office hours, need not attend office, and should not be bothered about designations; and where the CEO lets other people make nearly all the decisions. He mentions that in SEMCO, a Brazilian company where he is the CEO and majority stakeholder, despite this work style that seems to be a recipe for chaos, its revenues have consistently grown. The company has recorded very low employee turnover.[60]

Semler explains that for those willing to take a chance, there is a better way to run a workplace. He laments the manner in which technology—laptops, cell phones, email, etc.—that was supposed to make life easier, has in fact robbed people of free time and destroyed the traditional nine-to-five workday. When you have the freedom to get your job done on your own terms, and to infuse your work-life with enthusiasm and creative energy, you will become more productive.[61]

Fulfilment

Unless we open our mind, we will continue to deceive ourselves. In my years of consultancy, to begin with, I have been impressed by senior executives, individually and as a group, be it for their attire, their eloquence, their determined and at time vociferous articulations, and their dedication to their organizational commitments. However, the first impression almost always had to be corrected later. The pride they demonstrated in their position and responsibilities slowly disappeared as our personal relationship grew stronger. The more trust I built, the more they opened up. This helped them reveal that the erstwhile glowing presentations about their work were not entirely true.

---

[60]Emler, Ricardo, 'One: Any Day', *The Seven Day Weekend: Changing the Way Work Works*, Portfolio Penguin, New York, 2004, p. 13.
[61]Ibid., p. 42.

Gradually, I heard stories of their anxiety, frustrations and stress. Some would make genuine but self-defeating statements by saying they may be able to find happiness once they have made a certain amount of money and then do social work or community service. Obviously, these desires would remain a 'wish list' for many until their superannuation. Satisfying organizational commitments is the main hurdle to fulfilling family commitments. A number of research studies have undoubtedly reaffirmed the strong correlation between organizational justice and commitment, and personal stress.

Many of us equate a job with money—a blinkered perspective indeed. This, coupled with hyper-consumerism, causes people to chase material wealth, neglecting the work-life balance—the bedrock of life. With work taking over many peoples' lives, if the work-life balance is not maintained, it may lead to work–life conflicts, stress, and the onset of myriad diseases at a young age resulting from long hours of work, and an ever-increasing workload as discussed earlier.

The concept of a model employee of the recent past has steadily been discarded in today's context. The new crop of executives, especially from Gen Z, has questioned the work ethics once followed by the older generation, their working style, loyalty and organizational commitment and their long years of service in the same company.

To the discomfort of many Baby Boomers and Gen Xers, the emergence of the new breed Gen Z will willy-nilly transform the work landscape. As more and more Baby Boomers leave the workplace, leaders from Gen Z will replace them. We have witnessed Gen X and the millennials already occupying many senior-level positions supervising Baby Boomers. Their work and lifestyles may not be aligned with those of the elders. For example, loyalty to the organization and staying for a long duration in the same organization might be the core values of Baby Boomers, but the following generation, especially Gen Z, is least inclined to stay in the same organization for a long period.[62] The emergence of new work values, ethics and attitude has given rise to more conflicts among multigenerational cadres in their day-to-day transactions.

Today, a major challenge for the HR department across organizations is handling disputes between senior workers and freshers, in their interpersonal communication and over getting work done; since fresh college graduates assume the role of supervisors, they may find it difficult to handle experienced, senior workers due to certain incompetencies.

The predisposition of each generation breeds more adversaries than collaborators. A general complaint I hear about Gen Z is that they are not willing to work extra hours or on weekends, and they care little about building themselves as future leaders in a company.

The lack of awareness about each generation and their context gives rise to more interpersonal conflicts, especially in the workplace. Gen Z is more interested in *creating* new things rather than *leading* others. Guided mainly by technology, their communication style is short and crisp. Gen Z already makes up for twenty-five per cent of India's workforce; and their reports with emojis have become a

---

[62]'Engaging Gen Z BB 2025', *greatplacetowork.in*, 17 March 2025, https://tinyurl.com/4sufv69j. Accessed on 5 June 2025.

normal part of their digital body language. Also, digital body language for them is a crucial form of workplace communication and a key to building bonds.[63]

It is imperative for industries and employee engagement teams to sensitize the elders and senior management executives to certain key characteristics and behavioural patterns of Gen Z, and vice versa. Most Gen Z expect flexibility, autonomy and purpose-driven organizations. Today, many companies are revisiting and redrawing their recruitment/selection policies, performance matrix, and employee engagement, among others, in meaningful ways. Hierarchical fiefdom is giving way to consensual deliberations.

One of the major concerns faced by industries across India today is attrition. Though there was a decline in the attrition rate immediately after the pandemic, the trend has reversed. The attrition rate in IT services firms is slowly inching up.[64] Many industries have an attrition rate of seventeen to twenty-eight per cent due to many factors: concerns about organizational culture, inadequate compensation, and limited scope for learning and development, to mention a few. Hence, it is essential, for industries to examine closely this new thinking and questioning, emerging expectations and aspirations of Gen

---

[63]'Can emojis aid workplace communication?' *The Hindu,* 4 June 2025, https://tinyurl.com/2pr5mtsh. Accessed on 5 June 2025.

[64]Kannan, Uma, 'IT firms see increased attrition rate, global capability centres more attractive choice for talent', *The New Indian Express,* updated on 16 May 2025, https://tinyurl.com/m5u2a4vz. Accessed on 30 May 2025.

Z as a cohort, to create a stress-free work life. While many companies have initiated strategies to retain people, there is still a long way to go.

While many organizations are trying to get a grip on addressing the challenges in handling Gen Z by evolving new strategies, a whole new gamut of physiological and psychological problems has been cropping up across generations. The changes brought about have simply not produced enough positive results in terms of our well-being.

While work from home is seen as a perk offered by the management, it has not yielded the desired results. While the comfort of working from home is the primary selling point for some companies to retain people, oftentimes employees prefer working from office. The distractions for an employee and the family while working from home are manifold, and become a breeding ground for discord among family members.

As expected, women are the worst affected, more so since in the Indian set-up, domestic chores are still predominantly handled by women. Men still prefer giving women feedback rather than sharing the domestic workload, compounding an already difficult situation for women.

Adding to this, electronic gadgets play a huge role in restricting family interactions and communications. Consumerism compounded by easy offers, life-on-credit may ensure a physically comfortable life but at the cost of neglecting both our psychological and emotional needs.

It is well established that most adults suffer adverse health effects from stress and a large percentage of all lifestyle diseases can trace their origins back to stress. For organizations, this type of work-life disbalance results in low productivity and an increased attrition rate. The implications are highly detrimental to one's well-being. Greenback Cat hostages are particularly predisposed to facing marital discord.

Unlike our Western counterparts, Indians are resistant to seeking professional help for their mental/psychological issues. The largely peaceful and close-knit family set-up in India is steadily becoming a thing of the past, due in part to competition and consumerism, and in part out of the desire to emulate the West in many spheres. While there is nothing wrong in emulating the West, it doesn't always bode well for a country like India.

Integrating family, work and personal life requires self-awareness, deep reflection and deft handling. Family bonding remains a priority as does spending adequate aspirational time and energy to look after the needs of the family. The lack of quality time with the family takes a huge toll not only on one's well-being but also on the well-being of the family. While some of us may be good at cultivating and maintaining family ties, others may shine at work. The important thing is to never let one take precedence over the other. Handling both family and work in an equitable manner and with effectiveness is much desired. In the long run, happiness at home and a decent personal life are key determinants of a successful career.

Paths VI and VII: Stress and Health

I have combined stress and health as they are correlated, deeply affecting each other in their contribution to one's well-being.

Human beings can never escape stress; it was and will remain a natural reaction each time we sense danger (in any form) or are faced with a problem. Our ancestors had to combat animals and other natural disasters and when they saw or sensed danger, their bodies were conditioned to kick into gear. Hormones elevated the heart rate and blood pressure signalling them either to fight or take flight.

Today, the threats or dangers we face are inherently different from those of our ancestors, the resulting stress being far heavier and in many cases, life-threatening. Instead of wild animals and unknown environmental changes, our stress is replaced with psychological, economic and social threats. We have spouses, bosses, children and targets to meet, all lined up in an imperfect symmetry. We can't run away from them; instead we have to literally and figuratively face them every day.

If we are in a conference or in a meeting, a chance question from the speaker directed at us can make us break into a sweat. This 'eustress' can be considered to be beneficial as it can propel us to perform. But when such stress becomes chronic, it can manifest itself as a physical ailment. We are aware of how stress kills by way of heart attacks, high blood pressure, diabetes and lifestyle diseases, among others. A hapless few are even driven to suicide.

Young entrepreneurs and the corporate community in India were shocked to hear of the untimely death of V.G. Siddhartha, founder of Café Coffee Day. Although the cause of his death is debatable, it has largely been attributed to stress brought on by his mounting financial troubles.

Here was a person who had created more than 50,000 jobs and a strong brand, but admittedly wrote in his alleged parting letter (the entire letter is in the public domain), 'I couldn't take any more pressure.' While this example is not to pique anyone's morbid curiosity about one man's internal struggles, it is to highlight that life and work are filled with learnings, which we sometimes fail to understand.

Whether or not V.G. Siddhartha was a failure as an entrepreneur as he believed himself to be, is beyond the scope of our discussion. I would only like to appreciate the lessons he has left us in his wake:

- Life is transient with its share of crests and troughs.
- Success can't be defined by power, money, empire, etc.; nor can the absence of power, money, empire imply failure.
- Leaving 'a sense of belonging' to create 'belongings' often boomerangs.
- Stress is the biggest killer.
- One may walk into a hostage situation voluntarily.

Take a break! Work stress can lead to serious ailments and in extreme cases, to early death. Work-related stress is an ongoing problem; volumes and tomes have been published on its causes and possible remedies. Unfortunately, this knowledge has hardly made a significant impact on any workspace or professional set-up, the prime reason being the widespread acceptance of stress as part of the work culture. I have seen many a résumé that includes 'highly stress-tolerant', as though that is a requirement to be gainfully employed.

A job or work must enable a human being to lead a healthy and productive life. A healthy job is likely to be one where the pressures on employees are appropriate in relation to their abilities and resources, to the amount of control they have over their work, and to the support they receive from people who matter to them. The World Health Organization (WHO) in their constitution defines health 'as not merely the absence of disease or infirmity but a positive state of complete physical, mental and social well-being,' and states that 'a healthy working environment is one in which there is not only an absence of harmful conditions but an abundance of health-promoting ones.'[65]

In a study conducted by The Canadian Nova Scotia Health Survey, researchers examined the association between 'positive affect'—feelings like happiness, joy, contentment and enthusiasm—and the development of coronary heart disease over a decade. They found that for every one-point increase in positive affect on a five-point scale, the rate of heart disease dropped by 22 per cent. While the study doesn't prove that increasing positive affect decreases cardiovascular risks, the researchers recommend boosting your positive affect by making a little time for enjoyable activities every day.[66]

---

[65]'Constitution of the World Health Organization,' World Health Organization, https://tinyurl.com/45xcfnt5. Accessed on 13 October 2025

[66]Davidson, Karina W., et al., 'Don't worry, be happy: positive affect and reduced 10-year incident coronary heart disease: The Canadian Nova Scotia Health Survey,' *European Heart Journal*, Vol. 31, No. 9, 2010, pp. 1065–1070, https://tinyurl.com/twwkkeuk. Accessed on 2 June 2025.

Path VIII: Inner Harmony

Attaining inner harmony is the ultimate endeavour of an individual in the grand journey of life. For some it is a longing, for others it may be an ornamental utterance and for others still, it could well be the philosophy of life itself. How many do truly enjoy the fruits of inner harmony? Not being serious enough about it and focusing superficial attention on inner harmony could also contribute to failure for several people.

Attaining and sustaining inner harmony is by and large a work in progress. It is akin to cleaning our house each day, getting rid of the cobwebs and dust that have accumulated over the years, and eventually putting things in order.

I prefer to rephrase the words 'inner harmony' with a more simplistic term—'sense of balance' in life. This may sound a bit more achievable (it most certainly does to me!), rather than the heavyweight 'inner harmony' which can set off abstract speculation, although in spirit both remain the same.

As economic challenges increase, most of which are self-created, there is a gradual giving up of ethics, values and health. This undeniably leads to more inner conflicts, which we either allow to fester in our minds or we wage a war within ourselves to make the honourable choice. Rest assured, those who wage the right war often find a way to maintain a balance in life.

Steps to Reach Inner Harmony

While inner harmony and peace can certainly be attained,

they can only be attained gradually, and not overnight. The following steps may help you attain them:

1. Identify the source of discomfort: Probably the best example would be of fresh engineering graduates from colleges in India. Their saga is painful and pathetic. The hope to land jobs with fat pay cheques immediately on graduation drive them to pursue an engineering degree without any other goal (thanks to IT companies). Many remain unemployed due to their poor operational skills and the ever-oscillating market demands. Many fail to assess their employment worthiness. They continue to live in the world 'as it should be' rather than in the world 'as it is'. Lack of awareness of the ground reality only contributes to prolonged periods of unemployment as these young people let up the opportunity to gather precious work experience, and end up facing an even more challenging environment.

The more sensible ones analyse the reason for their discomfort and understand that the source of this discomfort is not really unemployment or underemployment. Instead, it is their own poor self-worth and unpreparedness to shape themselves into effective, constructive professionals.

This can be further corroborated with another example that many will recognize from their own experience. An employee is told off by his boss, 'I have tolerated enough, this will be the last time. Pull your socks up!' Once he returned home, his wife correctly guessed that his pensive face was the result of some unpleasant experience, and enquired, 'Anything wrong in office?' He surely would have preferred if she had asked if everything was alright. Unfortunately, she caught him in a rather vulnerable moment. Feeling cornered, he assumed (incorrectly) that she expected a rundown of all that had transpired at work, and started to defend his behaviour, while his anger flared up (for no good reason), leaving his wife to bear the brunt.

Such incidents are common in most families and often culminate in a mix of anger, guilt and frustration. The irrational reaction brings on a rush of adrenaline that often clouds one's judgement, in turn wrongly laying the blame for the reaction elsewhere, and creating further frustration and discomfort. A faulty identification of the source of anger, guilt and frustration will lead to the obfuscation of the problem, leading to more complications.

2. Offload your status and power: We have already discussed how misconceived 'status and power' can cause misery. Being transient in nature, power and status come and go with positions and designations. Being addicted to or obsessed with status and power in the workplace can only impact others, mainly subordinates, negatively. In my understanding, and I am sure many share my point of view, this is not a desirable quality in a leader. A leader has to inspire others. Effective leaders with high self-esteem hardly use the power that stems from their position, or even aggression, to get things done. While each position in the hierarchy comes with its own power, how one wields this power makes all the difference. Subordinates usually obey their superiors mainly due to fear of the consequences of disobedience. Moreover, their obedience also stems from the notion that the responsibility for the consequences rests with the superior who ordered them to do what they did.

The well-known Stanley Milgram Shock Experiment[67] tested obedience to authority, and his agency theory offers more insights on the issue. Milgram explained the behaviour of his subjects by suggesting that people have two states of behaviour when they are in a social situation:

- The autonomous state, where people direct their own actions and take responsibility for the results of those actions.
- The agentic state, where people allow others to direct their actions and then pass off the responsibility of the consequences to the person giving the orders. In other words, they act as agents for another person's will.

Milgram suggested that two things must be in place for a person to enter the agentic state:

1. The person giving the orders is perceived as being qualified to direct other people's behaviour. That is, they are seen as legitimate.
2. The person being ordered about is able to believe that the authority will accept responsibility for what happens.

Have we not experienced how some of our superiors conveniently passed the buck to their subordinates when things went awry? Do their actions justify their power and status? That is the pitfall of being in a state of agency.

---

[67]McLeod, Saul, 'Stanley Milgram Shock Experiment', *Simply Psychology*, updated on 14 March 2025, https://tinyurl.com/5bvz7m4s. Accessed on 30 May 2025.

It is not my objective to discourage those who want to climb the corporate ladder in order to seek status and power. Aim to be in a state of autonomy. Remind yourself that chasing power and status will demand a heavy trade-off, with very high chances of one's inner peace being a casualty.

One can earn one's status through more prudent means. There is something to be said about growing at one's own pace, irrespective of position and authority. This internal growth can never be taken away by anybody at any time. This is what makes it all the more inspiring—both to the self and to others.

3. Need vs ostentation: A rich man was asked the following question, 'How much is enough?' He replied, 'Just a little more.' Need and greed are relative in their quality and quantity. Need can include a spectrum. For someone, owning twenty pairs of shoes to wear for different occasions can be a need, whereas simply owning two pairs of shoes can also be construed as a need. Need can be equated with the basics of life and is pretty much self-explanatory. Greed, on the other hand, is generally defined as an excessive desire to possess and display one's symbols of wealth, power and status. Excessive means possessing and displaying something harmful to the self and/or to others. A particularly apt example can be a treacherously greedy politician or landlord who tries to amass wealth either through coercion or corrupt methods. Similarly, if a workaholic's aim is to make more money at the cost of personal discomfort and family discontentment, this will also fall under greed. While this topic can always be discussed with some saying each to his/her own, in a society, this does not always bode well for others. It is reasonable to feel that as long as we live as 'individuals', but when it comes to a bigger picture involving the society, when one person takes more than his/her share of the pie, it irks everyone else around, creating social conflicts. This is equally true for families with the absence of work-life balance.

Inner peace is not the outcome of being poor; it is the outcome of our outlook and attitude towards life. You can be rich or poor. Today, a manager with a family of four needs a car and a decent-sized home to live in comfortably. By way of inheritance or through corporate perks, if one ends up with a luxury car, well, enjoy it! Yet, if your lifestyle is centred around or determined by branded items and obsessive buying only to display your wealth, it may land you and/or your family in deeper trouble—psychological or otherwise.

Many acquaintances are permanently struggling to manage their lives, all due to the foolhardy lifestyle they have become used to. Unpaid loans piling up, increased pretentiousness and self-imposed aloofness are some of the problems they constantly face. As millennials and the middle class increase in India, a majority of them are particular about owning a car, a property and maybe some investments in gold. The ground reality, however, is different; both spouses work hard during their prime, losing their youth in the bargain.

The desire to own a home has become a fundamental aspiration, particularly among the younger generations in India, driven in part by the decline of the traditional joint family set-up. While housing affordability is usually assessed through factors like income, expenses, and property prices, these aren't the sole concerns. In reality, the way individuals manage their spending can also reflect in their ability to afford a home. Unlike their parents, who benefited from a time of economic stability and growth, today's youth face a more uncertain future. Experts caution against the risks of multi-generational home loans, noting that while it's important to meet essential needs, it's equally vital to recognize the fine line between necessity and excess. When that line is crossed, it often leads to stress and instability.

While their parents enjoyed a period of unprecedented peace and prosperity, the younger generation is looking at a future increasingly fraught with uncertainty. While needs should be fulfilled, one should learn to draw a line between need and greed. Greed invariably leads to anguish, incertitude and stress.

Club Ninety-Nine
Once upon a time, there lived a king who, despite his luxurious lifestyle, was neither happy nor content. One day, the king came upon a servant who was singing happily while he worked. This fascinated the king—why was he, the supreme ruler of the land, unhappy and gloomy, while a lowly servant had so much joy? The king asked the servant, 'Why are you so happy?' The man replied, 'Your Majesty, I am nothing but a servant. My family and I don't need much— just a roof over our heads and warm food to fill our tummies.'

The king was not satisfied with that reply. Later in the day, he sought the advice of his most trusted advisor. After hearing the king's woes and the servant's story, the advisor said, 'Your Majesty, I believe that the servant has not been made part of the Club Ninety-Nine.'

'Club Ninety-Nine? And what exactly is that?' the King inquired.

The advisor replied, 'Your Majesty, to truly know what Club Ninety-Nine is, place ninety-nine gold coins in a bag and leave it at this servant's doorstep.'

The king did as told.

When the servant saw the bag, he took it into his house. When he opened the bag, he screamed with joy. So many gold coins! He began to count them. After counting them many times over, he was at last convinced that there were ninety-nine coins. He wondered, 'What could have happened to that last gold coin? Surely, no one would leave ninety-nine coins!'

He looked everywhere, but that final coin was elusive. Finally, exhausted, he decided that he was going to work harder than ever to earn that gold coin and complete his collection.

From that day, the servant's life changed. He was overworked, horribly grumpy, and castigated his family for not helping him make that hundredth gold coin. He stopped singing while he worked.

Witnessing this drastic transformation, the king was puzzled. When he sought his advisor's help, the advisor said, 'Your Majesty, the servant has now officially joined the Club Ninety-Nine.'

He continued, 'Club Ninety-Nine is a name given to those people who have enough to be happy but are never content, because they are always yearning and striving for that extra "coin", that little more, telling themselves, "Let me get that one final thing and then I will be happy for life."'

4. Cease the fear of the future: Being able to envision the future is a potent strength. A few people envision the future for themselves and for society at large. A country must think of its future in terms of its population vis-à-vis its infrastructure, environment, health, education, etc. So must an individual. No one is devoid of expectations, although spiritually we are advised to think otherwise. It is wise to think and plan for our future, right down to the career we want to choose by assessing our passion and commitment and by improving the quality of education that we offer our children as part of our future. However, our struggle arises when we spend considerable time ruminating about our past and future out of our fear of uncertainty.

Mark Manson, a self-help author, was asked by someone about the extent to which unattachment needs to be taken seriously, be it with people or with belongings. The person continued: 'If I didn't think of the past and the future, wouldn't I become an irresponsible person? Will unattachment be possible in a demanding world?' The pertinent question here, according to Manson, is, 'If I am supposed to be attached to nothing and desire nothing, how the hell do I get anything done?'[68]

[68]Manson, Mark, 'The Zen Dilemma', *Mark Manson*, 7 January 2014, https://tinyurl.com/5f9n2rcr. Accessed on 30 May 2025.

That seems like a logical question to me, and raises our common concern. Manson proceeded to clarify the doubts of the person. The mail below was his response.

The problem comes with the explanation of attachment. Many people take it as wanting or desiring anything. This is where we see people living in communes, giving up their possessions, and moving to religious retreats. The catch is that actively being unattached to things is still being attached to something. You are attached to being unattached! Actively desiring to be desireless is still a desire!

A more proper explanation would be that it refers not to just something that you want or desire, but rather to things you are afraid to lose. In life, everything is lost. Everything. At some point, everything goes away, and therefore, to have anything at all, we must be willing to accommodate that loss. "Being present" isn't ignoring the past or the future. That's impossible, because the act of thinking about a past or a future is actually taking place in the present. It's impossible to not be present. What changes is how you identify yourself.

It's about widening your perspective, expanding what you identify to be a potential part of you. Recognizing that you have such little control and little knowledge of, well anything in the world, that you might as well let go and be humble about it. Have your career goals, thoughts and ideas, your hopes and dreams, but don't attach the self to it in such a way that you'll suffer if you don't achieve them.

Culturally, Indian parents are concerned about their children's future. So concerned that they earn, build a property portfolio for their children, and mount a lavish wedding for them too only to satisfy others. They are never satisfied just providing education and allowing them to step out of home. Barring a few, most parents end up living for our children's future rather than for their own self. This to me is a serious question to consider and address. While that is easier said than done, we need to question ourselves on whether we need to change or continue to deprive ourselves of our inner peace?

5. Inner harmony: Inner harmony is a feeling of peace of mind that involves self-acceptance, acceptance of one's life in general, and acceptance of the past. Understanding oneself is the precursor to self-acceptance. Self-acceptance is unconditional; it is about accepting our strengths and vulnerabilities. It is about completely embracing ourselves with respect to our attitude and aptitude.

If by way of attitude, one has a bad temper, and an unpleasant demeanour while dealing with others, does that qualify for self-acceptance too? Let me explain further. I've observed that when confronted with failures or mistakes, people often tend to defend themselves or attribute the issues to external causes, rather than reflecting on the feedback provided.

Self-acceptance in the above context involves two parts: the first part is, understanding one's unwanted or inappropriate behaviour and accepting the same since it has been perpetrated by the self. Part two is, what are we going to do with that acceptance? Stop or change? Suppose someone stops at part one and concludes that since they have accepted their behaviour unconditionally, they can now think of it as the end of the matter and make their peace with it. However, this attitude will invariably lead to problems in his/her interpersonal relationships. Will it not lead to distrust and unwillingness to change? As adults, we need to exercise prudence when responding to others, especially with people in our circle who matter the most to us, when they point out our objectionable behaviour. While it is vital to listen to their point of view, it is equally important that we don't victimize or brand ourselves as 'inadequate people' and that we cultivate our mind positively. When it comes to counselling, counsellors often follow the dictum 'Accept people as they are.' It is equally applicable to the self: accept yourself as you are, however do not stop at that; move on—towards bettering yourself. This will only lead to inner harmony and peace.

Aptitude-related inadequacies exist in all of us, and could vary from person to person. While the acumen to negotiate with colleagues may be lacking in a manager, he/she may prove to be better at other managerial skills.

People with self-acceptance will leverage their strength while those teetering on non-acceptance may blame themselves due to their own self-doubt or develop prejudices based on external insinuations about or perceived comments on their vulnerabilities. Either way, they fall into a trap, a trap mired in myth.

In a country such as India, the command over English plays a consequential role. Countless executives possess excellent functional and cognitive skills, but struggle to reach any sort of pinnacle in the corporate sector due to their lack of proficiency in English. The inability to speak English fluently is more of a deep-rooted malady than a simple issue of learning or mastering a new language. Executives too have inhibitions and many a time, feel they are unworthy of/inferior in a group where a good communication flow is determined by how well one speaks English. The corporate structure in India and the employees in general need to be sensitized to this and periodically be reminded of all those folks who were able to break the glass ceiling by hardly using the English language. This attitude of self-acceptance also means to liberate ourselves from being hostage of our own captivity. It will also encourage others to be as they are without being either prejudiced or judged critically.

We may understand self-acceptance to be a great succour when it comes to getting rid of our guilt and self-flagellation. We must have the courage to accept both our strengths and vulnerabilities with equanimity. That is the way to build self-esteem, the right path to inner harmony. Without self-acceptance, our psychological well-being will suffer, and we will end up getting sucked into a maelstrom of constant stress and anxiety. As the external world degenerates into a toxic habitat, socially, psychologically and environmentally, we are left with only our own selves to work on for inner harmony. In that sense, I reiterate 'inner harmony' is simply an internal state that permits us to be at peace and emerge confident, even in the face of adversity. We must resist the urge to run after material wealth, power and status. Rather, our task should be to remove ourself-created barriers, cravings, aversions and biased views. We need to be sure of what we are chasing after. If we are too stuck in the past or busy pursuing the future, we will miss the present altogether.

We are led to believe happiness arises out of different experiences. We all want to travel, move to a different city or country, seek out more variety in every sphere of life. However, if our present self is innately unhappy, our future self will also remain unhappy, regardless of the sheer range of accumulated experiences.

Epilogue

We have two lives, the second begins
when we realize we only have one.

—CONFUCIUS

The following quote aptly sums up most workplace scenarios: 'You are killing yourself for a job that would replace you within a week if you dropped dead. Take care of yourself.'

We may all have a multitude of excuses for allowing ourselves to become hostages. What we fail to realize is that performance from a sense of our self-worth is different from performing to prove unto others. The deer often outruns a tiger in the forest. That is probably the only way it can reassure itself about not becoming the tiger's prey. On the other hand, tiger has to outrun deer to have its meal. While this analogy is used in seminars conducted for sales executives, it does nothing more than encourage them to achieve the higher targets. But our imagination is what will determine who is the tiger and who is the deer among the people present.

While this analogy inspired me initially, of late I have

found it bewildering. Are we in a forest? Do we take that to mean that our workplace is set in the wild? Are we mere animals in search of prey for our survival or are we preys ourselves? Against such a backdrop, the term 'head hunting' takes on a whole new meaning.

The constant, consistent stress to perform better is nothing short of a death knell. Being effective does not have to mean being stressed out. It is our responsibility to lead and live a life of happiness. As employees, we must strive to identify the most suitable organization that believes in and practises corporate ethics and transparency, and places a premium on employee well-being too. While this combination may be hard to come by, the lack thereof should never compel you to either choose or remain in the wrong place.

Acknowledgements

When I started writing *Corporate Hostages,* I recalled reading a research report on 'Corporate Prisoners' that was published under the title 'Releasing Performance: The New Agenda for HR' in 2009 by Chiumento[69], an HR consulting group based in London. I take this opportunity to thank Chiumento, as their paper provided the practical cue to the broader framework of this book.

Many thanks to my daughter Kavya Raj for her patient reading, and her understanding of my ideas and of the structure of this book. Her recommendations helped shape the syntax, style and content immensely. But for her, my writing may have delivered less. As a reader and as a budding writer, she helped me focus on the book and on its themes whenever I digressed. For that, I shall remain forever grateful to her. I would also like to express my sincere gratitude to Karpagam, my junior from college, for her immense support in editing my manuscript.

Thanks to Rudra Narayan Sharma from Rupa Publications for commissioning this book. Thanks are also due to Arjit Sharma, whose editorial inputs played a

[69]*Releasing Performance: The New Agenda for HR. New Thinking for HR Professionals.* A Chiumento Green Paper, Chiumento, 2009.

significant role in lending coherence to the manuscript.

Above all, I would like to thank the many executives who have been participants in my numerous organizational development intervention programmes for sharing their accomplishments and their struggles. Both are now part of this book.

Bibliography

'Business Case Studies on Forced Labour.' *International Labour Organization,* 1 Aug.–31 Dec. 2010, https://tinyurl.com/ynknptpk. Accessed on 6 May 2025.

'Can Emojis Aid Workplace Communication?' *The Hindu,* 4 June 2025, https://tinyurl.com/2pr5mtsh. Accessed on 5 June 2025.

'Constitution of the World Health Organization.' *WHO,* World Health Organization, https://tinyurl.com/45xcfnt5. Accessed on 13 October 2025.

'Foresight Mental Capital and Wellbeing Project: Final Project Report – Executive Summary.' *The Government Office for Science,* 2008, https://tinyurl.com/38y32dxe. Accessed on 6 May 2025.

Adorjan, Michael, et al. 'Stockholm Syndrome as Vernacular Resource.' *The Sociological Quarterly,* vol. 53, no. 3, 2012, pp. 454–474, https://tinyurl.com/mrx2k438. Accessed on 30 May 2025, p. 457.

Amnesty International. 'President Trump's First 100 Days: Attacks on Human Rights, Cruelty and Chaos.' *AmnestyInternational.org,* 30 Apr. 2025, https://tinyurl.com/2judfy8v. Accessed on 30 May 2025.

Arcadis. *The Arcadis Sustainable Cities Index 2024: 2,000 Days to Achieve a Sustainable Future.* Arcadis, 2024, https://tinyurl.

com/4u6je8jc. Accessed on 5 June 2025.

Bachard, Charles, and Niki Djak. 'Stockholm Syndrome in Athletics: A Paradox.' *Children Australia*, vol. 43, no. 3, Sept. 2018, pp. 175–180. Cambridge University Press, https://tinyurl.com/2zan634u. Accessed on 30 May 2025.

Bakhtiar, Abbas. 'Global Economic Outlook: 2012 and Beyond.' *The Market Oracle*, 23 Feb. 2009, https://tinyurl.com/yyx86nps. Accessed on 6 May 2025.

Bhutani, Chetan. 'Unacademy, Byju's IAS, Drishti IAS among 20 Coaching Institutes under Scanner for Misleading Claims: Sources.' *Business Today*, 23 October 2023, https://tinyurl.com/4re42zu2. Accessed on 2 June 2025.

Bird, Jim. 'Work-Life Balance Defined.' *Worklifebalance.com*, https://tinyurl.com/4p27nwj8. Accessed on 5 June 2025.

Boseley, Sarah. 'Unemployment Causes 45,000 Suicides a Year Worldwide, Finds Study.' *The Guardian*, 11 February 2015, https://tinyurl.com/3scepx52. Accessed on 2 June 2025.

Briscoe, Jon P., and Douglas T. Hall. 'The Interplay of Boundaryless and Protean Careers: Combinations and Implications.' *Journal of Vocational Behavior*, vol. 69, no. 1, 2006, pp. 4–18, https://tinyurl.com/4d6hhhda. Accessed on 3 June 2025.

Carmody, Bill. 'Tony Robbins: Success Without Fulfilment Is the Ultimate Failure.' *Inc.com*, 11 Sept. 2016, https://tinyurl.com/yc4fvr9b. Accessed on 6 May 2025.

Cantor, Chris, and John Price. 'Traumatic Entrapment, Appeasement and Complex Post-Traumatic Stress Disorder: Evolutionary Perspectives of Hostage Reactions, Domestic Abuse and the Stockholm Syndrome.' *Australian & New Zealand Journal of Psychiatry*, vol. 41, no. 5, 2007, pp. 377–384, https://tinyurl.com/4swtrnkv. Accessed on 30 May 2025.

Chiumento. *Releasing Performance: The New Agenda for HR. New Thinking for HR Professionals.* A Chiumento Green Paper, Corporate Prisoners, 2009.

Cole, Devan, Katelyn Polantz, Ramishah Maruf, and Elisabeth Buchwald. 'Appeals Court Strikes Down Many Trump Tariffs, but Delays Enforcement until October.' *CNN International*, 29 Aug. 2025, https://tinyurl.com/ar5mm54b. Accessed on 30 August 2025.

Davis, Bob, and Elffie Chew. 'IMF Chief Says Nations in "Depression".' *The Wall Street Journal*, 9 Feb. 2009, https://tinyurl.com/46t2wrxz. Accessed on 6 May 2025.

DeFillippi, Robert J., and Michael B. Arthur. 'The Boundaryless Career: A Competency-Based Perspective.' *Journal of Organizational Behavior*, vol. 15, no. 4, 1994, pp. 307–324. Wiley, https://tinyurl.com/4de46yu2. Accessed on 30 May 2025.

De Vries, Manfred F. R. Kets. 'Seven Signs of the Greed Syndrome.' *INSEAD Knowledge*, INSEAD, https://tinyurl.com/c6c2bekw. Accessed on 6 May 2025.

Development Bank of the Philippines, and Frank Radstake. *Philippines – Second Local Government Units (LGU) Urban Water Supply and Sanitation Project: Resettlement Action Plan. Vol. 1: Policy Framework on Involuntary Resettlement and Compensation for Land and Assets.* Development Bank of the Philippines, 2005.

Emler, Ricardo. 'One: Any Day.' *The Seven Day Weekend: Changing the Way Work Works.* Portfolio Penguin, New York, 2004, p. 13.

ET Online. 'Is 90 Hours a Week Legal? Here's What Indian Labour Laws Say about Working Overtime.' *The Economic*

Times, 20 Jan. 2025, https://tinyurl.com/3jfmxaen. Accessed on 30 May 2025.

Firestone, Karen. 'Why That Risky Career Move Could Be a Safer Bet Than You Think.' *Harvard Business Review*, 11 Mar. 2016, https://tinyurl.com/4vwtzed8. Accessed on 6 May 2025.

Hall, Douglas T. 'The Protean Career: A Quarter-Century Journey.' *Journal of Vocational Behavior*, vol. 65, no. 1, 2004, pp. 1–13, https://tinyurl.com/39uuthrb. Accessed on 2 June 2025.

Henkel, V., P. Bussfeld, H.J. Möller, and U. Hegerl. 'Cognitive-Behavioural Theories of Helplessness/Hopelessness: Valid Models of Depression?' *European Archives of Psychiatry and Clinical Neuroscience*, vol. 252, no. 5, Oct. 2002, pp. 240–249, https://tinyurl.com/3fk5vc7z. Accessed on 6 May 2025.

Higgins, E. Tory. 'Promotion and Prevention: Regulatory Focus as a Motivational Principle.' *Advances in Experimental Social Psychology*, vol. 30, 1998, pp. 1–46, https://tinyurl.com/5c6phu79. Accessed on 6 May 2025.

Imranullah, Mohamed S. 'High Court Frowns upon Use of Orderlies by Police Officials.' *The Hindu*, 20 Mar. 2018, https://tinyurl.com/437swdve. Accessed on 30 May 2025.

Kannan, Uma. 'IT Firms See Increased Attrition Rate; Global Capability Centres More Attractive Choice for Talent.' *The New Indian Express*, updated 16 May 2025, https://tinyurl.com/m5u2a4vz. Accessed on 30 May 2025.

Kim, Yoshiharu. 'Current Perspectives on Clinical Studies of PTSD in Japan.' *PTSD: Brain Mechanisms and Clinical Implications*, edited by N. Kato, M. Kawata, and R. K. Pitman, Springer-Verlag, 2006, p. 149.

Lama, Abraham. 'PERU: Tale of a Kidnapping—from Stockholm

to Lima Syndrome.' *Inter Press Service*, 10 July 1996, https://tinyurl.com/45k5kce5. Accessed on 30 May 2025.

Lewis, Michael, Jeannette M. Haviland-Jones, and Lisa Feldman Barrett, editors. *Handbook of Emotions.* 3rd ed., Guilford Press, New York, 2008, pp. 294, 666.

Maslow, Abraham H. 'A Theory of Human Motivation.' *Psychological Review*, vol. 50, no. 4, 1943, pp. 370–396, https://tinyurl.com/2htuwmwt. Accessed on 30 May 2025.

McLeod, Saul. 'Stanley Milgram Shock Experiment.' *Simply Psychology*, updated 14 Mar. 2025, https://tinyurl.com/5bvz7m4s. Accessed on 30 May 2025.

Nordt, Carlos, et al. 'Modelling Suicide and Unemployment: A Longitudinal Analysis Covering 63 Countries, 2000–11.' *The Lancet Psychiatry*, vol. 2, no. 3, Mar. 2015, pp. 239–245, https://tinyurl.com/yrvtvaxm. Accessed on 6 May 2025.

Sanvictores, Terrence, Navid Mahabadi, and Chaudhry I. Rehman. 'Classical Conditioning.' *StatPearls*, National Library of Medicine, updated 5 Sept. 2024, StatPearls Publishing, 2025, https://tinyurl.com/2sdk6wdv. Accessed on 6 May 2025.

Senge, Peter M. 'Chapter 2: Does Your Organization Have a Learning Disability?' *The Fifth Discipline: The Art and Practice of Learning Organization.* Doubleday, New York, 1994, p. 17.

Senge, Peter M. 'Chapter 16: Ending the War Between Work and Family.' *The Fifth Discipline: The Art and Practice of the Learning Organization.* Doubleday Currency, New York, 1990, p. 306.

Toffler, Alvin. *The Third Wave.* William Morrow and Company, Inc., New York, 1980, p. 31.

U.S. Bureau of Labor Statistics. 'Employment Situation Summary of August 2025 – April 2025.' *U.S. Department of Labor*, 2 May 2025, https://tinyurl.com/4k7kczsc. Accessed on 6 May 2025.

Zuckerman, Marvin. 'Why Were the Nazis So Successful at Killing Six Million Jews?' *Jewish Currents*, 18 Apr. 2013, https://tinyurl.com/mr2eavj7. Accessed on 30 May 2025.